Mr. ByTheWay

His memories of four and a half careers and myriad odd jobs turned into an entertainment

Peter Davidson

Matador
9 Priory Business Park,
Wistow Road, Kibworth Beauchamp,
Leicestershire. LE8 0RX
Tel: 0116 279 2299
Email: books@troubador.co.uk
Web: www.troubador.co.uk/matador
Twitter: @matadorbooks

ISBN 978 1784624 460

British Library Cataloguing in Publication Data.
A catalogue record for this book is available from the British Library.

Cover design by Nick Theato

Printed and bound by CPI Group (UK) Ltd, Croydon, CR0 4YY
Typeset in 11pt Aldine401 BT by Troubador Publishing Ltd, Leicester, UK

Matador is an imprint of Troubador Publishing Ltd

MIX
Paper from
responsible sources
FSC
www.fsc.org   FSC® C013604

This book is dedicated to all those who gave even my most outlandish ideas the benefit of the doubt.

Thanks to all those that gave me permission to use the photographs.

PETER DAVIDSON

He has had success with four and a half careers and done several odd jobs.

As an actor his range was to appear in films by Polanski and Hitchcock as an extra and eventually got full film credits.

His first part was in a way his biggest. It was 'Say No to Europe' by Marion Read, in a "circus" setting. He played the entire Common Market Agricultural Policy when not being Wales etc. His dressing room was the third step of the fire escape at The Oval Roundhouse.

All this was a far cry from a Merc. limousine ride from the dressing room to the temporary 'swamp' at "Pinewood" with Anthony Hopkins as a travelling companion (Great Expectations) which came later.

His lecturing goes from an invitation public lecture at the National Gallery which led the Director to give him carte blanche in The Gallery, to teaching at a South London comprehensive (supply) and as a Spoken English specialist both in France and for the BBC World Service.

He came to tourist guiding after these things because he developed an excited interest in it and was ultimately elected a Fellow of the Guild of Guide Lecturers. He showed French MP's round the Palace of Westminster, firemen from the North East of England round London and conducted the curatorial staff from the Museum of Ethnography in Manitoba round the British Museum as well as very specialised trips round galleries and general sightseeing tours in French and English.

A tale to tell…

He founded Magic Carpet Productions in 1982 and it has now produced a mixture of spoken word cassettes and DVD's adding up to over 50 titles – all received well. His 'An Invitation to Contemporary Art' has been sold at Tate Modern consistently for 20 years. See the advert at the back of the book for details.

His short story 'The Recital' was broadcast by LBC as the winner of a national short story competition. He had a poem published in the first issue of the pan-British universities magazine YOU.

Odd jobs include, honestly, dishwashing (Whiteleys, Queensway), assistant sales person in a hardware dept., waiter, several lorry drivers and encyclopaedia salesman and translator.

These memories have been brewing for a long time and are now ready for drinking.

Dear Reader,

Mr. ByTheWay by Peter Davidson

…is not presented in chronological sequence.

It's rather that, on a rainy day, I've entered into the spirit of the thing and jumped gleefully from puddle to puddle – trying to make as big a splash as possible – instead of teetering around on safe ground.

Hope you approve.

Peter Davidson

CONTENTS

CHAPTER I

THE BEGINNING
– CHESHIRE.

A crosswind blew along the dunes causing a formation of planes to veer in unison – Wellington bombers. They were taking off to head to the dunes square on, over the Irish Sea to "Europe".

On the crest of the dunes were two boys looking for secret footpaths among the sand at the top. As the planes drew nearer, their noise filled the air – this raucous drumming. They waved energetically at the first one for they could see perfectly clearly the pilot in his loosed off flying helmet. He waved jovially back. So it was – all the pilots waved jovially until the last one which coincided with a chill descending as the sun slipped away. They turned and slouched down the now shaded slope of the dunes to home, making the noise – the snarling drumming made by a Wellington Bomber, with their arms outstretched.

It was good to be one of those boys.

My father was in the army and we had rented a room in "Rossnyger" on the island of Anglesey where he was doing manoeuvers. It was worth it for the furtive waves at him on exercises or marching past our window with the other soldiers.

That's about my only recollection of the War since I was born in 1939. There was a hint of combat when I was two – I was told much later by my mother – we were walking where I was born in Cheshire, probably to the British restaurant renowned for its whale meat sausages, when a German plane came up behind us, strafing the pavement. My mother was quite young at the time but found adrenalin from all over the county to scoop me up in her arms and jump over the nearest hedge and plummet into a living room, as she put it "in the excitement of the moment – and I didn't even know the people, Peter." I must have been about 2 and thus I was spared.

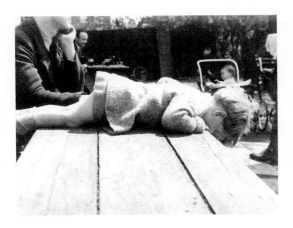

Childhood Photos

So my souvenirs of the War are my father's souvenirs – my father's gifts to me. After the Duration, his medal ribbons, his sergeant's stripes and a greatcoat mackintosh bomb shelter sort of cape – ah – which was not at all breathable and brought you out in a sweat which lost you a stone after about five yards of walking in it. Eventually, this was given to the church in London where the tramps would gather for such treasures. And memories of childish things because it was wartime and because it was my childhood – childish things like, best of all, the sledge that my father had knocked together with bits of wood and strips of metal and we went to a quarry at the top of the horizon behind the house and there we came down – would you believe it, my father in his army boots steering magnificently, my mother sat in her best slacks and me perched on top, scared to death probably. We finished up in a snowdrift but we were 'Happy Families' and it was worth it for that.

I found an incendiary bomb (casing I hope) in the wasteland by the quarry and triumphantly brought it home and kept it in a drawer – I hoped it hadn't gone off or, rather, had gone off before its transhumation to our house. We had a shelter in the big room we had. We lived in a semi-detached house, pretty well rent free – it came with my father's civil service job – sort of two down and two vaguely up. When asked what class we were, my father immediately replied lower middle class and my mother said upper middle class. It was like an episode of Keeping Up Appearances.

Anyway, there we were, perched in the middle of semi rural suburbia but within sight of the Liver Building and the Liverpool Docks a couple of miles away as the Luftwaffe flies. So we were obviously a target in that house and eventually moved out for me to live with my grandmother and my cousins in Derbyshire.

CHAPTER 2

'EVACUATION' TO COUSINS IN DERBYSHIRE.

I was at most 9 when I left Cheshire and went to the primary school in this mining dormitory village where you could see the pitheads from my window, but apart from lorries going up and down the road outside, filled with coal deliveries from the colliery and the miners who had finished shifts squatting against a wall with their white neck scarves as if an inevitable habit had possessed them, it was not very much to do with mining. Mining is more a tradition than a fact. My grandfather, for instance, began as a coal miner on 4d a day before becoming a coal merchant and pit owner until stopped by a fault in the geology. People came out from time to time picking up lumps of coal that had fallen off overloaded lorries certainly, but it was a green field situation once you crossed the road – a meadow where I fired the bow and arrow my father had kindly made for me; where I, in the little pond, floated my metal sailing boat which my temporary Uncle Bill had made (who sadly succumbed in the War in the RAF – his plane crashed on take-off. He was the bomb aimer and the crew daren't approach him 'because they had just one big bomb onboard… was this the Dambusters?') He realised it had no keel so slopped on its side.

So I went to him, mercifully holding it with a piece of string but he melted lead into the keel and it sank like a stone – so much for his aeronautics.

More later, more later.

This house where my grandparents lived at one time with their six children to me as a small boy appeared like one of those palatial almost villas where the gentry lived in black and white films. It really was an almost baroque version of D.H.Lawrence's house in "Bestwood" as he calls it, two up two down and there he was with his family plus me and my mother. How on earth they lived together passively I don't know. It may have been the inscribed piece of wood that was above the dining room table which said "Home is the place where we grumble the most and are treated the best." Unless that was truly taken to heart, it must have been hell at times. Anyway it was companionable. My cousin lived across the little yard. It ran onto what was, for the time, an enormous garden which was given over mostly to vegetable cultivation but at one time housed a pig ('Angie', the name) which finished up on the slab in the cellar and mushrooms which produced an enormous crop. They made this "breeze block" sty mushroom farm themselves in the garden.

So it was a rich, rich environment for me as a boy running amok.

The bit at the bottom was used by the powers that be to strip bomber engines down at the end of the War with beautiful ball bearings for catapults as I thought all over the place.

It became my coal merchant uncle's storage yard with loading machines here and there but the whole thing was a hotchpotch of delights for an adventurous boy. I remember working for Tom (my uncle the coal merchant) for a week, expressly to get myself a Parker 51 pen which gives you an idea

Derbyshire – With my cousins.

of the date. This was successfully done. It was a helluva lot I must say, lugging hundredweight sacks of coal around at that age but I was able to do it and it may have paid off in other ways. It did make me discus champion of my university but all that's to come.

So this baroque villa was my habitat for one of the happiest times I have had, playing football with my cousin Jim who became a very good footballer – played for Derby County – scrumping of course, building dens, playing knickknock and setting off fireworks all over the place and generally, as I said, running amok, without constraint really. I attended the local primary school where everybody was in love with Vera Reilly. Vera Reilly had copper hair cascading over her shoulders and the boys virtually fought to sit behind her and be enraptured by her. It was all very chaste.

I remember infantile cavortings in a flashing direction when I was in Cheshire. Apart from that, the most exciting thing that happened to me in Cheshire I think was to be on the hills that came down to the Mersey on the Cheshire side eating our weekly pocket money's worth of buns and bats and chewing gum and – what was that pink thing with a minty flavour like a stick of rock – like a bar of chocolate but pink with a minty flavour? There we were wallowing in gargantuan pleasures and, would you believe, as promised, the Bristol Brabazon flew down the Mersey. It was an extraordinary sight which I will never forget. It had a tail fin like a regatta, four engines – yes, 4 engines – on each wing. Absolutely immense. It was like a whole squadron of aeroplanes with enormous power in reserve flying down the Mersey with an uninterrupted view and running buffet for us – quite an experience!

Otherwise, experiences included going to the Tatler in Liverpool – a little cinema for Saturday morning films – being scared to death by the Scorpion and digging the cowboys and Indians and so on. It was a good time – and the scouts came into that period, the cubs as well. Playing tennis already – quite well – at the local courts with my parents, playing cricket on the waste ground behind the house, setting fire to hedges – all sorts of excitements in Cheshire. I was pleased to be there but, as I've said, the interlude in Derbyshire was particularly nice. Nothing to think about really except being comfortable, extremely comfortable in my primary school where there was no corporal punishment, a lot of encouragement which set me up for the next phase... and Vera Reilly!

One thing I did bring from Cheshire – I still don't recollect how – was a ginger pussycat which my father brought home when we were in Cheshire, in his greatcoat – a beautiful little cat which we called Tiddles. And Tiddles got pieces of fish that

I went looking for like the Holy Grail down at Hartley's in the shopping parade. So he got bigger and bigger and bigger. I mean it – twice the size, three times the size, four times the size till he matured enough to bring down a swallow on the lawn and was put into solitary confinement in the garage for a period – as long as I could stand it really – then released. But relations were a bit cool after that although we got him, somehow, to my grandparents' house where he roamed around and got coal dust all over himself, like the rest of us. Due to his manslaughter of the swallow , we renamed him Tiger and he lived up to his reputation as if to the manner born – he was a monster, weighing it seemed several stone and did 0 to 60 like a Ferrari.

CHAPTER 3

ESCAPE TO THE FARM
IN LINCOLNSHIRE.

The next move was a great trek from Derbyshire to Lincolnshire, to a farm in Lincolnshire – from a vaguely industrial empire in Derbyshire. Bill, the airman had been engaged to my mother's sister and over time the two families had become close so it was suggested I should live on this farm for the time being so my mother and I set off – but how did we set off? We were transported from Derbyshire to Lincolnshire in Tom's Coal lorry! With bits of furniture here and there in the back and me. Also an ex –army water bucket containing the mighty Tiger securely pinned in so he would come to no harm. Off we go! It's a very long way between the two places and when we got there, entering this enormous farmhouse kitchen, Tiger was released and he honestly leapt straight through an open window onto the lawn. He was quite clear about his feelings. Socially, he was never seen again except via rats left on the doorstep occasionally but he could be seen from time to time against the skyline at dusk closing in on a wolf, bison or even an elephant perhaps '?' He just disappeared into that farm environment which was to him vast. I'm sure he was much better off and felt much more free than he had done hitherto.

I too, in some sense, went back to nature on the farm. I had my sandwiches for lunch with the gardener for instance and I mucked in generally. I remember a fox running perilously close to me in a wheat field and going out with a local lad to snare with a rabbit snare a pike motionless in a dyke – hunting – quite big. We put it on a meat plate and left it in an outhouse. I don't know why but it was swept away by Tiger, one presumes, beautifully finished from the tail forwards, ramshackle but systematic – no use to anyone thereafter.

So, home produced everything to eat you could imagine – very, very good and wholesome family meals around this enormous table and general atmosphere of pleasantness. I was living, I suppose, with the landed gentry, you could say. They really were. The farmer himself, now fairly old, had been captain of England's hockey team, for instance, and generally was thoroughly respected as far as I know throughout the country, let alone the county.

I used to go shooting. I went from an air rifle to a 410 and shot the fauna right, left and centre, an action I'm still rather ashamed of. One does that sort of thing at the age of 12 or so, I believe. My mother and I drove a herd of pigs from the station, the railway station about a mile away. It took most of the afternoon by the time we learned pig herding. But I'm forgetting the most important thing of all in a way. My dream of having a dog was satisfied. While Tiger was leaping through his window, there lumbered from an enormous armchair a Labrador retriever aged 3, saying hallo on principle, banging everything with its tail – you wouldn't believe the enthusiasm. His name was Chantry AND he was my buddy for the time it took to be a boarder in this farmhouse. Fantastic!! This made everything seem right as you can imagine. He played hide and seek with me. Can you imagine playing hide and seek

Lincolnshire – Chantry.

with a retriever? But I did – I told him to count to 100 while I disappeared between two haystacks and then called "Chantry" and he'd come slowly but surely round everything you could imagine until he would zoom to find me in my hiding place. Great days, great days. I spent a lot of time pushing him out of dykes, totally undisciplined but the soul of affection I can assure you and thoroughly enthusiastic. I think I invented "walkies" before Barbara Woodhouse. We'd go tramping across the road adjacent, over the fields and little bridges and so on to the next parish which was, honestly, about 2 miles away and then I would whistle him back which he ignored completely but eventually we came back home after an enormous walk really which felt like nothing at all – it was so enjoyable.

I attended the local primary school which seemed very focussed and I was beginning to realise that it was a professional matter to be a pupil at a good school so worked very hard. I remember outside the school as such I entered a painting competition and painted a quarry which got a commendation of some sort so that was rather nice, wasn't it? Powder colour was the medium of the day. This school also had a Vera Reilly in my class! But this time she was a brunette and like what I imagine the young Elizabeth Taylor would look like. Anyway, she was loved from afar by everyone including the form master who made her undisputed teacher's pet although he did the best he could to conceal it.

Okay, so much for romantic interests.

I suppose you could say it was pretty well idyllic. I remember going as a beater for a shooting party on the farm dressed as I was in my juvenile outfit which incorporated short trousers and unfortunately found nettle beds right left and centre, as I eagerly followed the other beaters. I was nettle rashed all over the place. Then it began to drizzle and that exacerbated the irritation. It was bloody awful and I whimpered all the way back I remember. It was a 'permanent' nagging pain as it seemed but it did mark my transition to long trousers which was a rite of passage.

But it was eclipsed by a bad day at the cricket ground. They were one short and I was asked if I would play. I was very very young but a good bowler I must say (5 wickets for 8 runs – name in the paper – playing for Hull Y.P.I. vs Smith & Nephew – elastoplasterers to the nobility) so I turned up in the best shape I could, that is, above all, plimsoles which of course slipped on closely mown grass. Well, I promise this is true – in the throw-about before the match began, I hit the incoming batsman on the back of the neck. Once there, I was asked to bowl. I was so intimidated I bowled short off-breaks about 4 feet from the batsman just right for a 4 (he duly obliged). Of course I dropped a catch and was out for a duck. I remember slouching off the field at the end and seeing a boxer dog trying to find a gap in the 'wicket fence' to join his master on the steps of the pavilion, brow furrowed as only boxers can and this general feeling of consternation. If I'd been old enough I'd have said to it 'I know just how you feel, duckie.'

Horrible, horrible – a blot on the landscape, as they say. Of course, I was out for a duck. All this is on the County Cricket Ground. So, attempted murder, a dropped catch, about 36 runs given away for nothing and out for a duck – not good. It was an eye opener or should have been I must say, but an understanding of the old English idiom: "to be out of one's depth."

Meanwhile, a precocious youth I felt by then was growing up. The 11 plus was not mentioned as such but I did pass it and had an interview at a medievally established grammar school which I also passed and before you could say Boadicea, I was bounding along to my new destination and new school as a boarder, in a Land Rover pursued for at least a mile and a half by a lolloping Chantry no less until something else required his attention.

CHAPTER 4

BOARDING SCHOOL: 7/10.

The prospect of going away to a boarding school was exciting. I was going to wear a uniform, meet all sorts of people I had not met before, do all sorts of exciting things I'd read about in books, in comics and so on. Need I say there was no television at this time so the expectation was untarnished by knowledge.

The first two or three years were very good. One was being brought forward with new things and was generally for it. I remember buying badges to do with the school and things like that. Slowly I worked myself through what was available. It was quite an enterprising school I should add. It had a very good teaching staff. Because I had done well in the 11 plus, I was consigned to an upper stream where we did Latin rather than a lower stream where they did woodwork and art. It's a source of regret that I didn't do art as well as Latin. There was a certain amount of mobility between these courses I must say. I remember being relegated to the lower stream for Maths for a time, which I was traditionally bad at and then my Uncle Bill – temporary Uncle Bill – helped me revise before my 11 plus for instance – and I remember hating double maths on Thursday morning.

However that's the way it was. I used to come more or less

in the middle of the class, always very good at English, hopeless at Maths as I said and round about for the other subjects.

There was a boy transferred from the local secondary modern into our Lower Sixth form with success, so it was enterprising and quite liberal in that sense. There was no bullying that I could remark on, no homosexuality to speak of or at all. I can remember kissing a boy because his mouth was like Brigitte Bardot when I was about 15 but that was the extent of it as far as I know.

I worked myself through the agenda – captain or vice captain of all the teams, colours equally, house captain, senior house boarder, school prefect incidentally and so on. I had my fair share of punishments even in the Upper Sixth, as head boarder for 'romping' with a bright kid that I got on with exceedingly well in the form below me. He was punished too once the light dawned that we were just mucking about. In the later stages of the school, I had a room of my own and that was a blessing to work when I wanted to, listen to the radio etc. – it was a liberation.

On the lighter side, I was stopped with a mate of mine cycling in my pyjamas up the road in the middle of the night by a police car. We explained we were from The School and he said 'Right, off you go.' They understood. We went for a midnight swim stark-naked. As far as I know nobody was caught but that was the 'frisson' of it of course.

I remember taking my swimming trunks off in the middle of a swimming session taken by the Headmaster, as a dare to myself and not being able to find the bloody things until the very last second which was excitement in itself! You see the poverty of entertainment to which we descended really. To cap it all I suspect, there were what we called garage doors at the end of a couple of dormitories, including one that I was in at the time, round about Form 5. It was a beautiful summer night and the lavatories were at the other end of the building, so we 'pissed' outside through this garage door, this double window, in concert. It was rather a fine feeling – it might have been a sort of acapella if one of them hadn't been singing 'Knees Up Mother Brown' (I think it was) as we did it. You can imagine the experience for the Headmaster walking his coconut matting dog round the corner to find the beginnings of a fracking exploration with everyone focussing on this ever increasing hole among the cabbages. Anyway, he let us go on for a moment or two then made an appointment with us for after Assembly the next day, which was retribution of course, but the moment was dearly held. We played softball in our pyjamas till we were stopped. We learned ballroom dancing from a boy whose parents ran an Academy of Dancing until that was stopped and things of that sort. We were, paradoxically, let loose on a dance in the town to mark something or other and there I met the love of my life, in terms of swopping photos and clandestine meetings and so on until I was caught by the headmaster at the old folks home the choir had recently sung at, kissing my lady love – what's wrong with that? Anyway, I was gated for a term, had to plead to have a haircut, in the town of course.

Thus was the drama of my schooldays which I can't say I thoroughly enjoyed.

I came away with a couple of prizes: lower sixth English and upper sixth English. I said one line of Shakespeare in the school play, was in the school choir and sang in Lincoln Cathedral as part of the local church choir. I played rugby for the County, athletics for the County. Otherwise it was pretty humdrum. I think the best bit was the concerted "piss" out of the double doors, honestly. In fairness, I must say that was probably an exaggeration. There were moments but it was mostly an act of defiance on my part, and the perverted will to win etc. etc. – all the adolescent virtues. Perhaps the best moment – one of them certainly – was driving away our family Morris Minor after Speech Day (the final Speech Day) wearing the tartan tie of the Clan Davidson. I had become myself again! Good feeling!

There were sort of ancillary benefits – financial, Black Market, black economy I suppose. Pocket money was 1/6 in the lower forms and rose to half a crown in the upper sixth when you were possibly 17 or 18 and for picking spuds at a local farm, I believe you got half a crown for an afternoon. For singing in the church choir, you got 5 shillings every 3 months – £1 a year but this was real money when you consider that our teachers, our masters were paid £16 a week to start with.

Talking about the Black Market economy, one of my jobs was to hand out pocket money to the troops and I used to be soft hearted about giving them a little extra if they wanted it and I lost track of that a bit. Come the end of it all, I had to sell quite a lot of my sports kit to make up the difference, the imbalance. Anyway, I left with a clean sheet.

When I was 17, I think, during a rugby practice, there was a perfectly innocent accident in which I broke my ankle and spent some time at home for that to heal – in a plaster cast. When I returned, I persuaded the doctor to permit me to do any sport except cross country which was an abomination – so that was a good moment too. I honestly remember in a barn which was at the beginning and end of the rustic part of the course, playing cards waiting for the others on the outward journey and for those on the inward journey, then just joining in. This was not on competition day but just "go and do the cross country" time. So that was a step forward – no more cross country but plenty of rugby, football and everything else! A mixed bag, my schooldays.

One thing I did come away with was a passionate love of the work of Dylan Thomas who was found in the senior library, a sort of sixth form library kept in a cabinet outside the staff room. I read an enormous amount of his work there and when I left, four of the five book prizes I had were works by Dylan Thomas. I regret that I didn't record the poetry of Dylan Thomas at the time or thereabouts when I really felt like it. Because of copyright, I should have recorded them then and waited until the copyright ran out and released them then. But 'c'est la vie.'

One thing that was rather nice was that I was neck and neck with another boy in my class in the Upper Sixth for the French Prize. The master honestly couldn't decide between us so set us an essay competition which I won and was awarded the French Prize but my form master decided that, since I had a prize already and the other boy had none, he should have the French prize. I took this rather badly at the time and was delighted when the French Master collected our textbooks and quietly presented me with the book that was my favourite in the French course – tantamount I felt to the French prize. It was Le Grand Meaulnes by Alain Fournier.

When I went to the Boarding School, I was of course 11 and my voice was very much a treble, but more than that a top treble so I was able to sing really quite high notes but not reach low notes. I went through the same process as most people do, my voice breaking at about 14 which I guess was approximately when this photograph was taken (I'm on the extreme right in the same row as the choir master). I was doing sport as soon as I went to the school so the general fitness was good and the master said I had the finest breath control that he'e ever come across which was reassuring. I made my way through the ranks, becoming an alto, then a tenor but I must confess that, after I'd been singing in

De Aston School Choir/With my school mates.

the Parish Church Choir as an alto I suppose, I did find my voice difficult to control from that transition from the higher register to tenor – came over as a hybrid, took a lot of concentration but I did sing the Shakespeare Willow song at a musical evening given for all and sundry including parents and in choir festivals, in places like Lincoln Cathedral which was an exhilarating experience. All this had a tremendous effect on my speaking and performance voice. I did get some music lessons from a singer on the QE2 for a while which was a good help too. I tinkered a bit with my accent to make it generally understandable but I have taken it seriously. I did voice classes at the City Literary Institute which gave me a lot. It was very professional and various in its approach. So I tried to graft on some tools of the trade as you might expect. It's strange in a way but, although I had abortive piano lessons for a short time and did all this singing and choirs, that I never learned to read music or shall we say I was never taught to read music. The fact is it rather passed me by in the way that algebra did mostly and anglo saxon did entirely. The trick was to come in with the same note as the guy next to me a micro second after he'd started it and I didn't mean to do it in a way, but that's the best I could do and it worked to the greater glory. This is perhaps why I often find it easy to imitate people who are talking to me, sometimes provoking a swing in the direction of my ear but it's quite amusing – it's a joke shared and to impersonate quite a lot of people I find enjoyable and really quite simple. I think it has its roots in my service as a choir boy perhaps.

Arial shot of school.

This is a pilot's eye view of my school. It was founded, I understand, in the 11th century or a little later by a Norman Bishop – Tomai de Aston – and it doesn't look very much as if it was (Victorian Gothic 1863, Grade 2 listed 1984). However, in the very heart of the building there is a tiny room (well, relatively tiny) which was mine in my last year and very welcome. It's accessible from the main corridor but inside, it's sealed at one end and if you peer through the fanlight in this interior wall you can see there are four feet or so of something… who knows, it might be the Da Vinci Code or a letter written by Tomai de Aston but never posted. Founders Day is always commemorated with a ghost. One of the senior boys will synthesise luminous paint or something equally clever and process around the dormitories while his cohorts follow banging whoever they can with pillows – all far-reaching intellectual stuff don't ye know!

The next day is a service at Lincoln Cathedral with the higher-ups conducting the service which is, in retrospect, quite a noble thing. The school, as you can see from the building, had worn out its traditions somewhat. It's a job lot, this piece of architecture if that's the word. As I said, my room was at the heart of it but there were chemistry labs added on, bike sheds and a gymnasium where the choir photograph was taken – assembly room, play going, pretty well everything – talking of which, I did one line of Shakespeare while I was there. It was "Did you not tell me this fat man was dead?" You've guessed it – it was one of the plays of Henry IV with Falstaff in it – played by the English Master with great zest I must say and that was it. That was my dramatic experience, officially anyway. There was no sign of preoccupations to come at all at this point. I just did it, like you do.

This areal view is particularly evocative to me because one morning, just as we got up about 7, there was this incredible noise from outside and I went to see what it was – the main entrance you can see towards the right of this photograph and the whole sky was filled with a Vulcan. The pilot had clearly buzzed the school – it must have been an old boy – but the sight of the underbelly of this white Vulcan climbing vertically, far too close for comfort, was unforgettable. This is Lincolnshire with RAF camps all over the place – some of them very famous e.g. the Dambusters, the Falklands War planes. Indeed the Vulcans took off not very far from where we're looking over the shoulder of the pilot, a couple of seconds after I'd seen all he had to show me – momentous .

My father was an excise man – famous in song and story – and tended to follow alcohol of one sort or another around the country to do his job. So it was Liverpool then it's... I mustn't go into this for it goes on forever. But we finished up next on the Humber Estuary where I stayed for a short time immediately after school. I worked in a local brewery and was a waiter in a seaside resort not far away, went along the coast on my bike for a swim and then on a motorised bicycle and then a small motorbike belonging to my father and found myself an awe-inspiring girlfriend. We used to listen to classical music together and that kind of thing. It was a very tacit but very sincere relationship I think, definitely an advance on anything previously.

I played (sounds like a quote now) I played for the local football team and of course I was retired. I had no school to do. I wanted to get into Cambridge if I could and swotted for the entrance exam, scholarship rather, alongside everything. I hadn't been advised about this ambition and I think I went for the wrong exam – not just an entrance, but scholarship. Anyway I went down to Cambridge for an interview with a stinking cold. It's amazing how glacial the wind blows from the Urals through Cambridge and it gets you for certain, in this case an ill wind. I wasn't accepted but offered an ordinary place in two years time.

The next move was serious. IT WAS SCOTLAND!

CHAPTER 5

"GAP YEAR" IN SCOTLAND.

Take a deep breath. Can you not hear the pipes and drums in the background, the proud swish of kilts, trailing their sense of history.

The reason I make these hallellujahs is because, when I was a boy, although I was brought up in the Midlands, you would think my hero would be someone like Robin Hood, it was in fact Lochinvar, a Scottish hero. I am one eighth Scottish and I like to think it's a good bit. Ultimately I suppose I'm a Viking – came over, don't ye know, with the wolf of Badenoch, a savage man. Among other things he looted and pillaged and burned down churches and apparently Davidson which is Scandinavian is his line. After the Battle of The North Inch in 11 something or 9 something, there were only 11 or 9 Davidson's standing so we had a merry time for about 1000 years repopulating the Clan. We have a tartan which is lovely – black and dark green with thin red stripe through it – squares picked out on it, I should say. The first thing I did when I went to Scotland was to buy a kilt for £8.15 which fitted me perfectly and I went wearing that and some brogues, hairy socks and a sporran I picked up in a jumble sale with my clan badge proudly displayed on it and a Davidson tartan tie but an ordinary jacket. This is me all over. Drooped in the wrong places but never mind. I went to the Hall of Residence inauguration get-together with the ladies from the Women's Union and I spent most of the time on the sofa, sitting there politely, in "Commando mode", if you follow me, it didn't affect me but what effect it had on the ladies I have yet to discover. Anyway, there was this jingoism for Scotland. It was the first time I'd been to Scotland and it was in Autumn so everything was crisp and attractive. I went to Speyside on the River Spey, famous for deer hunting, salmon fishing and its ancient castles, including Castle Macbeth, not all that far away and of course distilleries. It really was a pageant, rather than a journey, as far as I was concerned. I was besotted with the idea of Scotland and my ancestry. I really was. My clan motto is Sapienter si Sincere – wisely if sincerely – and that, I would say, is the flag that I follow when the best side of me is following the flag. I was proud. I was oblivious to people sniggering at my bumpy hemline between my kilt and duffle coat.

Scotland Dinner Guests (extras)

At one stage, I rowed from Kingston to Hampton Court and back in 'commando mode'. It was probably the same day that I swam 'starkers' the Thames at Kingston and gently ploughed across in the early evening to a fisherman who was dourly contemplating his bait which would not move and when I got there he said "The last bloke who did that died of typhoid," so I went back in Olympic time, into the nearest pub with clothes on now and had a double Glenfiddich! So the circle was complete – I was perfectly all right and I'd swum the Thames. I remember years later seeing Bamber Gascoigne breast stroking around in the Thames opposite his house in Richmond and I said "You're taking a chance aren't you?" "No, it's much cleaner now," he said. So God knows what it was like when I ploughed across, breaststroke, mercifully with my respiratory tract above water. Happy days in many ways, happy days.

Thus, to assert my Scottish lineage, I competed in the Highland Games at Aberlour and, to my surprise to be quite honest, came first in the hop, step and jump as it had become, tossing the sheaf I did something and, by a whisker, I was 2nd in tossing the 20lb stone, a thundering great thing – (the Olympic shot weighs 16lb) just 2nd to a chap who took his coat off and, otherwise, had perfectly ordinary clothes on, including shoes with bits of Blakey's reinforcement here and there to stop them wearing out on the pavement. Great feeling. It was a Scott's Porage Oats man to come!

My kilt etc. was sold to a shot putter student at Glasgow who wanted to compete in the Highland Games. I hope he was proud to become one more survivor of the Battle of the North Inch. Naturally, I subsequently wore a supplied kilt many times for parts and commercials. The only time I wore one in earnest was Hunting Moss Bros. Tartan to give away a friend on her wedding day.

Later on, in my adopted country, I worked in a distillery (perfect antidote to an English boarding school). I made some friends, obviously, and the distillery used to shut down at night at 4 o'clock and the pubs were conveniently open with their darts boards and all facilities at that time so I used to wet my whistle with the lads most days. This was early on but there was a big culture clash. We all sat around telling jokes and things and a bloke sat down next to us and had a pint glass which had been smashed round the drinking rim pretty comprehensively and I was feeling pretty euphoric and I smoked at the time so nonchalantly, insouciantly, really without thinking flicked the end of my cigarette into his dustbin of beer, which I was sure it was. Well, he suddenly heard the skirl of the pipes etc. and was all set to do an autopsy on me. Mercifully, the mates I was with understood all this much better and calmed him down. In fact, if I hadn't bought him a pint right filled to the top tout de suite, as they say, who knows, they might have debagged him or something – something frightful, don't ye know! My God, that was a lesson, my heart was in my mouth. I could not believe that he prized this shattered pint, three quarters of… So I undertook research to allay my confusion. Hector Gillingham, in his famous book The Face of New Caledonia (out of print) puts it rather well "I have observed that in towns above the beginnings of the Northern Parallel, they have strange, tribal (one might say) customs. For instance, if you have a pint, you mark it by smashing it with the pub ashtray all round the rim, rather in the way that dogs cannot resist a telegraph pole. In fact, as Rhubarb Meadow puts it rather well, 'it's quite common for dogs to do this – it's a kind of inheritance of theirs, the early settlers in the purlues of that region certainly showed them how'. "I played football" for the local team which helped my understanding of things Caledonian.

It was a refreshing treat to play rugby for the County, Moray, out of Elgin after the 'rah,'rah,'rah of school. Let me show you what I mean: at school when I was vice captain of the first 15, I played at scrum half for the moment – a kind of nuclear idea which worked partially, literally half, but I got so fed up waiting for the ball to be heeled out that I actually explained my feelings in colourful terms to the pack that if they didn't get the ball heeled back soon, I'd come in there and select one of theirs for myself and get on with the game. This prompted a whistle which is probably still going on from the Housemaster/referee type of thing, wearing somebody else's rugby boots I suspect. Anyway, I was dropped for 2 weeks without explanation or guidance or pills or anything… just dropped for a fortnight, then I mysteriously came back in my old position of scrum half again. I was supposed to divine what was meant.

Contrast this with playing for Moray. I remember once we were playing against the Fleet Air Arm and a blizzard started in the middle of the match which caused one of the backs of The Fleet Air Arm to run with sidesteps and swerves and dummies and God knows what, absolutely fair and square absolutely slap bang into the post. You could hear the noise of it in Tokyo. He stepped back, wondered whether to punch the post on the nose and then wandered around, having apologised for interrupting the play, to find something to do. Vive la difference!

This must have been the rugby that my Father experienced as full back at his university. I remember him taking me on his knee in his study one day when 'the flamingos' were coming to be fed at the French windows and saying "Peter, one day you'll play rugby. Don't forget it's blood, snot and toenails, definitely not for the ladies." How right he was but what an antidote to school rugby. What a great treat!

I should say that rugby remains the team game that I

most enjoy watching as a spectator. At heart, it's an intricate, clever game, full of intellectual pros and cons and so on. The physicality is really just a sideline and there are very few rugby players, in fact I personally have never met a rugby player who was malicious physically but I did see somebody foul someone, watching a match for Hull Kingston Rovers and Harry Markham, who was built like a cricket pavilion shall we say, just stood still in the middle of the pitch and waited for the guy, the transgressor, to pass by and tapped him, as he thought in the middle of the back. Well, let's say he never did that again.

Rugby at its height is artistic, delicate, cerebral even and the physicalities are taken as read, as is Anglo Saxon in reasonable quantities, as a birthright – yes. However, top flight rugby players master these skills but also take ballet lessons which is not really surprising if you've seen mercurial rugby played at, say, international level. It's extraordinary. The ball's a funny shape but at its best nothing else is as bizarre.

Anyway, we walked over the hills in the silvery mist to dances, a gang of us and we 'exhuberanced' ourselves tremendously and delighted many of them by moving rather than dancing which is so prosaic, isn't it? I remember walking back with girls over the hills and in the silvery mists, full of good escorting intentions of course. You were in the country, away from street lamps and things, the star cover made you feel one of them.

CHAPTER 6

SCOTLAND AND STUDENT AT THE UNIVERSITY OF GLASGOW.

Once I was in Scotland, I was accepted by the University of Glasgow and I had an application into Aberdeen. I consulted with the local English master and he said "Go to Glasgow, go to the metropolitan, international university – the big idea rather than just up the road which was, I thought, rather more parochial to be honest. I suspect he had been to Glasgow himself. I duly went to Glasgow for a Freshers' Camp for new students to meet up together with staff and have a general introduction. This was extremely helpful. There were members of the various societies strutting their stuff in the hustings, I suppose. The Dramatic Society I remember – in particular this is where Maggie was reading Dostoyevsky – as I recall and I was smitten. That was the first time I clapped eyes on her so I'll tell you the whole story later. All the societies had some publicity for themselves. We really knew a bit better where we were by the end of it and we formed a kind of international brigade. There was a Welsh veterinary student and a Norwegian medical student among others who went around together. I remember seeing The Vikings with Kirk Douglas together for instance and thoroughly enjoyable it was – all very valuable indeed. There was another camp in the woods for the more outward bound sort of students – bits of mountaineering and skiing – things of that kind but we were fixed at the centre of the University itself and exposed to all these things.

Glasgow University was founded in 1451. Remember there were 4 universities in Scotland before there were more than 2 in England – Glasgow, Edinburgh, St Andrews and Aberdeen while only Oxford and Cambridge in England.

Very well set up and aware of itself, it was easy to follow the university path through the delights I must say. Edwin Morgan was one of my English tutors – the poet laureate of Glasgow – and Lord Kelvin had been an alumnus there, so a university of some prestige and dignity. There I was – President of the Dramatic society at the end of my first year, on the selection panel of the film society and, yes you've guessed, played football for the local team and played in goal for the first team once – incredible speed of the game and precision compared to the third team where I was first choice as I recall throughout my university career. For a football-mad city, that wasn't a bad achievement. I enjoyed that enormously.

I also, from the beginning, threw the discus with greater and greater effect until I was champion of the university in my final year, I think. I got a selection for the West of Scotland as a reserve for an athletics match but, thinking it wasn't going to happen, I had a curry. Then, of course, they decided I was needed so I gave my apologies – an unfortunate missed opportunity which I regret. However, it was enjoyable to have the sports dimension alongside the academic.

I was doing a general arts degree. But the most important thing in a way was my tutor suddenly decided I didn't have enough languages to get a degree, would you believe (that must have been in my 2nd year) and we decided between us that I

Graduation Day at Glasgow.

would study Italian ab initio (from the very beginning) and this was a most amazing thing. They gave me the University Assistant – an Italian native – for the first year and I did the Scottish Lower Leaving Certificate at the same time and, in the 4th year (my final year at university) I did the Higher Leaving Certificate and got a merit, simultaneously, with the degree course with a second Italian assistant and passed. I think that was very much to the credit of the university. One wonders if that sort of thing would be possible in the straitened circumstances of today for I will always be grateful for the enlightenment on their part.

Equally, when Maggie finished, she went for teacher training. When I finished with 2 years of French (same as her) we applied to go to France to teach English as a spoken language and both of us were accepted – a privilege usually reserved for honours students and we had done general degrees. So off we went having been married – and I have to get this right – on the 24th of July, NO, August (oh dear!) 1961 so we'd been married for a year when we went to France, having made friends with the French assistants.

I spent my very first term at Glasgow in a hall of residence which became more and more school like in its constraints and its (what I consider) artificial manners. I left that and took a room in a house approved by the university where some students were already staying, one of whom was a very keen actor and very good. He subsequently went into the serious theatre as director and theatre manager, if you like, producer – George Ritchie. Well, the bomb was dropped. I became a devotee of theatre.

I acted in 12 plays when I was there and directed a revue and conducted a Beatrice/Benedict love affair with Maggie. We sparked off each other an enormous amount so eventually we got married and we acted in many plays together like Epitaph for George Dillon – she was Ruth and I was George – Hedda Gabler, where she played the lead and I played Judge Brack.

Then we both moved to the house where I was and it was all very adult from then on. We were married at Maggie's home town so it was a typical Scottish wedding – all very tribal in that sense. It was the same guest list I should imagine pretty well as had been drummed up for her uncles and so on but we did have Maggie's best friend as her bridesmaid and a mate of mine was best man. One impressive thing was that the lady of the house at the farm where I stayed, really quite a long way away from Scotland – Lincolnshire – came to the wedding which was a very very nice thing for her to do.

Off we went and, believe it or not, we went to the Edinburgh Festival for our Honeymoon where we mostly saw plays – incredible : The Three Estates with Duncan Macrae, Faustus with Paul Daneman who I was later in a play with, Five Finger Exercise by Peter Schaeffer, Songs for an Autumn Rifle by David Hare and the Cambridge Footlights including Willie Rushton, as I recall, so we had a really rumbustious time. I hope I haven't missed anyone out. If I have, mea culpa. But we came back to resume our "careers" if you like. We'd ducked out of rehearsals of a play to do this and incurred the wrath of the director until it was realised we had come back word perfect i.e. ahead of the rest of the cast so that was expiation enough.

It was a tumultuous bumpy time which was also pretty marvellous.

CHAPTER 7

FRANCE – TEACHING
SPOKEN ENGLISH.

Resuming the French journey: we were in Brittany staying with the French assistant and his wife whose marriage we had witnessed in the Town Hall in Glasgow – they didn't want to make too much noise about it in France. We were there for a week or so and he took us sadly to the wrong station but we managed to get from the goods only station to the passenger station in time and entrained with our halting, unaccustomed French speaking for the South of the country, discovering that Agen, where we went, was called Ageng to anybody who had ever visited the place and that if thirsty en route, you ordered une orangeade with that final e sounded if you wanted to get one.

So we found ourselves in this provincial but quite important town, where everyone asked us "did you eat the Pruneaux d'Agen" – the prunes in Armagnac which is of course a world delicacy and European mantra. But our minds were elsewhere as we seemed to parachute into this place. My first bit of conscious, fully focussed, on the ball French was to say to a cat perched on a gatepost of this little hotel where we stayed just for one night "what a beautiful dog you are. What a beautiful dog!"

(quel joli chien). The cat swore at me in rather sophisticated French I didn't understand but, by jove, I understood the intention. In we go to this hotel overnight and the next day discovered the one thing that was awry in our warm welcome – the accommodation generally. We spent the first few days in the sanatorium of the Lycee where I was to teach – the boys' grammar school if you like (Maggie had been appointed to the girls' grammar school in the same town which was unusual). It was quite common for married couples to be posted to opposite ends of France, only seeing each other at holidays so we were very lucky in that regard. However it's a bit close to the chest being in a 'dormitory,' above all with well meaning nuns kind of drifting around. Anyway, we were there. After that we slept on the sofa in the lounge as it were in a house where one of the English masters had a room. Then we went to – I was going to say local lavatory – but it was the local lavatory attendant's house we went to with a lot of improvised curtains. There seemed to be a lot of people in the house. It was very unnerving obviously, getting up for breakfast at the café across the road, having to hike over there half dressed. So we were feeling like refugees and then we got this house – ground floor room with an improvised shower, sink and cooker. The house was being refurbished. It was astonishing. The workmen came at 8 or was it 7 in the morning and blasted away but it was Valhalla as you opened your eyes. I'm sure it didn't do the nerves any good but we stood it for the time it took. At least we had a certain amount of independence, especially in the afternoon. I was leant a bicycle – the sort of camp bicycle –by the Head of the English Dept. He came around with us to try to find accommodation – you can't say fairer than that. He treated us to brandy snaps and four star brandy when we'd been to a rugby match with a chap we'd picked up on the way. The Captain of France at the time – Pierre Lacroix – was also the captain of Agen and PE master at the boys Lycee so everybody was a bit rugby mad, which was great. When England played France, we used to stand the French supporters a whiskey if England won and if France won we were stood an Armagnac by the same token – it was all extremely matey. We were plunged really into the society of the students who were supervising the pupils at the grammar school, some of whom were boarders, to earn a bit of money obviously to keep them going. So it was a jolly mixture. One had the company of the staff and also the student group as it were. We used to go to parties, dances, films, swimming – all sorts of things together in a random higgledepiggledy sort of way. It was very good from that point of view. I joined a local athletic club as an unofficial competitor in the shot and came second in the county championship, still euphoric from the party the night before!

The result was we very quickly learned a lot of French slang which was thoroughly enjoyable and also how much more exciting school dinners are in France than they are in England with the 'help yourself to wine' for supervisors and foreign assistants. We sat at the same table as the 'pions', as the student supervisors were called, with one or two staff mixed in as they felt and we talked about all sorts of things and learned a lot about France in a very convivial way. But the food – with the garlic especially – was really something and an enjoyable prospect to look forward to during the day. We ate lunch and dinner with coupons (Maggie came over from the girls' Lycee).

The first thing you do when you go to a school is compare it, as far as you can, with your own school. There really were significant differences. There was an abiding sense of organisation I was about to find out. There was a man, very much in his office, his department, looking after the food that was served, a man looking after the visiting students – the 'pions' that I mentioned, a man in charge of discipline – the censeur – and somewhere, beyond Mount Olympus in the Executive Class, was the proviseur, the provider, who was the Principal. No hint of any kind of physical punishment at all.

So the first thing we experienced was an abuse of privileges, as my first class filed past me, courteously standing at the classroom door, one of them said – not entirely under his breath, "You make me shit", in a phoney American accent. I'd never seen him in my life before and I'm sure he'd never seen me. It was just something he had to do. Well, I called down the vengeance of the Gods and put him in detention on Sunday via the censeur, which was the ultimate sanction. It was a boarding school but of course not all the students were boarders but the idea that this guy from a little village 10 miles away coming in to spend his Sunday doing Algebra instead of going hunting or going with his relations for a boozy picnic or whatever was not appealing but for me there was no middle course or I didn't know there was so it started off not very well but at least I demonstrated I wasn't a soft touch.

Teachers did not take registers for instance. That was the job of the 'pions' who accompanied classes from room to room as a kind of "don't even think about it" politesse. School started at 8 o'clock, which was already funny, till 4 o'clock when you cleared off, to do your homework no doubt if you wanted to do well. Sense of purpose in an all boys school I'm guessing of 500 people and quite a big staff of course supported by 'the pions' so socially good to be mixed in with the teachers and the supervisors and drink wine with them 'a toute heure' more or less any time it appeared which was any meal.

So, to have them let loose to do some free range acting was surprisingly very simple, We had pupils (I still prefer to think of

France – The foreign language assistants – Spanish assistant (Xavier), Me, German assistant (Alexis), Inge, Maggie and our Physics Master.

Bald Prima Donna by Ionesco – Play with senior pupils, plus me and Maggie on sofa. Directed by Xavier.

pre-university students as pupils) some from the girls grammar school, so to speak, where Maggie was teaching, some from the boys grammar school where I was, mixed together directed by the Spanish Assistant, Xavier Abril de Coo, and away we went. The result was very creditable. The Press thought it was very very worthy indeed and genuinely entertaining. Just to remind you, it was Jary's 'Ubu Roi' and Ubu the King in that was played by the Physics Master, to give you an idea, and 'La Cantatrice Chauve'(The Bald Prima Donna) by Ionesco, where there are 2 couples. M. et Mme. Smith which were played by 2 pupils from the two schools and M. and Mme. Martin, played by Maggie and myself. In the photograph you can see us on the sofa, really suggesting we were some kind of marionettes, whereas M. et Mme. Smith possess tremendous aplomb, the senior pupils they weren't mucking about. They were, if you like, extremely professional. They were very dedicated in what they did and there were no egos flying about at all.

The production was put on in the municipal theatre and also at a town down the road, called Villeneuve sur Lot (Lot was the river) and it went down very well. We got the usual slightly inflated reviews but the people did "venez nombreux" – they came in numbers. The theatres were pretty well packed as we did this. It was a tremendous experience and the first time I personally had been on a professional stage for instance. It was a good thing to do, in front of a big audience like that and in a foreign language – rather fulfilling and opened the eyes of the student body generally. I remember going to see the Headmaster and asking if we might do another one but he prayed, as he put it, for a "calm end of year" so that was that. But we did have little cakes and things and a cup of tea with him and his wife in his apartment in the school. He had graduated somewhere in English but never uttered a word of it, yet was benevolent enough. I mean he must have turned a blind eye to all sorts of misdemeanors pedagogically speaking – so all in all not bad.

★ ★ ★

I feel one of my 'gleeful puddle jumps' coming on.

Some years later, Maggie directed it for the French society of the University where she was teaching and I played the other husband from the one I played in France. It wasn't difficult to learn the new part. It's quite a gift. I don't recall parts after they've been used on the stage, unlike a lot of actors, the result being it's quite simple to learn something very close to what you've done without confusing. This production was distinguished by yet another stupendous performance from the "pulpit" by Maggie. The prompter was quite magnificent and bilingual. The other thing was Erica Cattle who appeared under licence from the One and Only Company (She was to be one of the pretty girls in The Importance of Being Earnest – more of which later) and now turned her talents to playing the 'maid' – an amazingly truculent character. It was suggested she might put a ladder in her stocking to show how casual she was and disregarding of any orders so she came back for the next rehearsal with what looked like two spiders webs but not matching and would probably be occupied by an octopus. It was an absolute miracle of cobweb, head to foot as it were. Fantastic – so she remains a pillar of the acting community for that. She went on, in spite of some people's fears to get a 2.1 in French and immediately got a job as Head of French in a school I believe and made her mark straightaway by dressing, out-dressing the pupils for vivid display. Good on her!

While I'm on these technicalities, I've never been prompted to my knowledge – ha! – except once when I was acting on a tour with a man who was a bit like these guys that pose as a statue with a tin for contributions. His acting was 100% inert but you had to avoid it – he was there! He was like a hologram. Anyway, I was fed up in a cartoony sort of way with this triumph of matter over mind and for my last speech as I remembered it, I swore at him (it was a vituperative speech but I swore to him at the end – sotto voce – in excellent gutter German). He nearly woke up but I threw myself for quite a bit of the play as a result… you're allowed **one** mistake, one mistake.

End of puddle.

★ ★ ★

Back to France:

The one thing that I failed at I think, to my dissatisfaction, was the teaching of the pupils themselves. I hadn't had any teacher training and it really was an uphill struggle for me and not always genial, although often so. I remember at the end of a section of the course asking the class in English what England was like. Then I helped them by mentioning places they had been told about or would know and got as far as Cornwall and the anglophile par excellence – a boy of 16 at the most – who wore an English blazer with a badge on the breast pocket and a striped tie, grey flannels with his hair parted on the left – a total anglophile – he said, honestly "pretty cliffy-yes-pretty cliffy" Eureka! So there was the occasional triumph. I remember years later, a'pere de famille' – very much the father of the family seeking me out with his wife and two or three children at the Tower of London explaining that he'd been a pupil in my class in Agen and finally got to London which he thoroughly enjoyed so I asked him if he spoke English most of the time and, need I say, the answer was a very eloquent gallic shrug of the shoulders and "mostly". I remember the Head of the English department when I went to his school saying that, apart from our most intimate moments, Maggie and I should speak French throughout our stay at the Lycee. He was of course right and equally the boy, well on the way to being a grandfather, was understandable. But there it is, you can't have everything. I did make a contribution. I read a thesis about contemporary Britain where I talked about the newcomers like Alan Sillitoe, John Braine and so on, the renaissance of northern realistic literature. We were all invited to do this. The Spanish assistant didn't turn up at all and the German assistant went down literally on one knee asking for the atomic bomb ('we're well behaved now')!

I showed some English films, including one with commentary by Stephen Murray, who I equally worked with later, about the ragged arsed crow talking about the landscape of Britain. He was surrounded by really good English voices so I showed that and it cost a bit of money from the British Council or the Arts Council but the pupils all chipped in their ninepence halfpenny or whatever it was and enjoyed them. The only bad news was when I took this bag of ninepence halfpennies to pay for my meals and the intendent (in charge of food) was not pleased. He had to be placated by the English master over time but all sorts of things to get used to – such as shaking hands with everyone all the time, things like that. It was an education in itself. The whole lot was a pleasure of the mind you could say and also of the body.

One of the most delightful moments of hospitality was when the English master introduced me to the local doctor who was very keen on things English so, fair enough, I went there and had conversations with him which lasted sporadically right through the school term. He was the son of farmers and I don't want to romanticise it too much, not exactly peasants I don't think but he had gone the other way and trained as a doctor and then as a surgeon. I used to go to his house and talk earnestly about various things but he would insist on taking us out for a wonderful Sunday lunch or tootling round the countryside but one thing I'll never forget, he'd completely refurbished a barn on the family farm. He'd lined it with marble panels and filled with old furniture – antiques I guess and so on and there at the magnificent table for twenty it seemed, he invited us to dinner which was wonderful and served by his aunties! It really was suddenly like being a member of the School of Athens. So very convivial. We had dinner and trips with one of the English teachers and trips with another English teacher. We were honestly fêted and accepted into the circle. So it was genuine that's the point and not a visiting academic, not at all. Rich times.

My medical pupil opened the door on one of the world's best kept secrets – the cure for the common cold. He had the beginnings of a cold so he took all the ordinary wine from his cellar, put on his English pullover and carried on as normal with the "everyday". Next day he operated, feeling as right as rain – a good way of curing a cold, if you can afford it!

We had a black market going nicely. I translated a text on diabetes for a doctor at the local hospital. The translation was done orally – a bit at a time – then we had one game of table tennis and drank single malt whiskey between times and he paid me for that! And I also taught a municipal councillor a bit of English so there was also that happening which all added up to my airfare would you believe to London where I was going for my Courtauld interview and thus we move seamlessly to a new locale for the time being.

The interview was in the awesome Courtauld Institute

which was then at 20 Portman Square – now a rather posh hotel I believe – and the Institute has moved to Somerset House basically right next door to Kings College, part of the University of London equally. My appointment was for the middle of the morning and I had the wit to spend the overnight in a hotel just round the corner so I woke up fresh, walked round the corner and overcame my intimidation of the place itself with its columns and marble, sailed up the Robert Adam staircase on the red carpet to a completely wood panelled it seemed room filled with Sir Anthony Blunt. Professor in State and, surrounding him, the top art historians of the world – thus it seemed to me. It was friendly enough I must say. They passed me things to talk about and so on, but I held my ground. I think I was very self possessed and I expressed the enthusiasm I had for the subject and my genuine desire to pursue it and of course I was all right when we got to Cezanne where we finished at Glasgow – Giotto to Cezanne and, as I explained to my Head of Dept. there, I wanted to know what happened next and he recommended the Courtauld. Otherwise I would never have heard of it. So it was all very happy and matey and I left there feeling quite buoyant to go and stay with my actor friend in Chiswick (from the same house in Glasgow) overnight, flew again to Bordeaux the next day and stayed at the apartment of the Spanish assistant so he's redeemed himself quite well by now and played football with him and his mates casually in a field beside the recreation ground with a dog the following morning and then slotted back in to life as it was, for this was term time at the Lycee you understand and, to be honest, thought nothing more about it. It was not an aggressive experience, the interview itself – not at all – very straightforward really.

A few weeks afterwards, I received a letter from the Courtauld at my residence in Agen. They said unfortunately the Modern

Period classes were full but they offered me the Baroque – I was applying for postgraduate studies in the Modern Period you understand. I wrote back and said I was very disappointed about this and would wait a year if necessary to study the Modern Period and he, Blunt, wrote back personally and said, 'We'll fit you in somewhere,' so that was the end of that but a nice act of benevolence.

Thereafter I knew him only as a teacher. He did seminars on Picasso with us although he was considered worldwide as a Poussin expert. He gave a lecture on Picasso's Guernica which began, 'Every time I approach this subject I realise how many friends I lost in that war. That was the only political utterance he made in my presence anyway and his tutorials were warm, probing and thoroughly delightful in an intellectual way. So when he was revealed to be what the tabloids called a traitor and was stripped of his honours, I was absolutely flabbergasted. There was no hint of that at all in the two years I was in contact with him. I shall always remember him as a majesterial figure, tremendous instant respect demanded in a very amiable way and I've heard not a bad word from anyone who was taught by him. So that was a really good experience.

CHAPTER 8

ODD JOBS IN LONDON.

When I came back from France I did some of my 'myriad odd jobs'.

I expected a bloke with a degree and a year's experience working in France i.e. with fluent French, would get a reasonable job relatively quickly. I traipsed round London until I finished up washing dishes in Whitely's in Queensway for ten bob a day, with an Indian lady of middle age as my colleague, who refused to confess to any knowledge of the Kama Sutra, although this was the sum total of my Indian small talk at the time. I didn't last very long there but found myself driving a lorry for a builder at Little Venice, carting bits of wood for the carpenters (the regular driver was in hospital) mostly around the Edgware Road end of Praed Street until I nudged a bloke who was at least 70 off his bicycle which had a high rise back seat of course and racing handlebars, at a leafy, sunshine mottled crossroads. As I said, I nudged him off his bike and got lumbered unfairly I thought by an incoming policeman. Anyway, I finished up at Marylebone Crown Court, was stared at as if I was a serial killer and fined £10 plus my licence endorsed. At least I didn't say 'he knocked me' when the summing up was done because he had this ungainly posture and no bell! NOTHING to warn me that this camouflaged bicycle was coming across my line of route. My boss was near the incident and offered the old boy a new bike but to no avail. Shortly after that I was replaced as lorry driver. I felt very wronged – the only explanation I can think of was that I'd been told to take some scrap metal and sell it for myself but instead of the nuts and bolts I took the lead next to them and made a handsome profit. Although I paid it back from my wages, it didn't do me any good.

I went to a lorry agency and had a lorry of quite big proportions with beer barrels on it to deliver to a club. And books, we were told in rifle shape wooden boxes taken from an embassy, which I can't remember now for convenience, to Northolt Airport where off it went in an RAF Hercules. It might have been the Encyclopaedia Britannica, who knows. I also learned a lot about South London thereby but I knew by then that I'd been accepted by the Courtauld so time was running out for this work experience if you like.

I finally worked as a supply teacher in a secondary modern school in South London where nobody, I was told, had ever passed any exam to do with English. Lo and behold, I was the French master! I fought back. I did the Geography course in 3 days (I failed Geography at O Level).

I remember doing a project called 'write me about a journey' using what you've learned in your English and Geography classes. One little fellow put on his paper, "Got out of bed, hurried breakfast, just caught the bus and arrived at school, in the nick of time". Wallop!

So that was one journey. Another one was marvellous. It was full of polar bears and elephants and hurricanes and God knows what until we got to the bottom of the page where he made a splendid scroll like a piano music stand and I just turned over out of idle curiosity – and it said, "AND SO WE MEET AGAIN."

I taught them rugby as far as they didn't want to do it. It was a pretty harrowing three weeks, alleviated, just about, by a

My first contact with television, 'The Blind Man',
Ravensbourne College of Art (student project).

free accolade. I was asked by a junior English master if I would like to join the tea club. 'They make the most excellent tea at the break time. Please, Mr. Davidson come and talk to us, join in,' this is all in a Bengali accent or thereabouts. Off I went and had this sinecure between the lessons which I stumbled through. At one stage, the bloke next door had to come in and execute a couple of people in the front row "pour encourager les autres"(to keep the others in line).

I did receive that year's Duke of Kent Award for distinguished service in lower education. This was on the back of receiving the invitation that ambitious parents put their children down for at birth – to join the tea club because, "The woodwork master makes excellent tea." Say no more.

I remember one of the teachers there was an Oxford graduate and wanted to put something back and I remember him cleaning his teeth at the end of the school day once, on his way to interview Alfred Hitchcock for a prestigious monthly magazine which made me think, "what had I done to help other people along, lower down the ladder of careers?" I certainly did help in acting. There was a sort of set-up where, for nothing at all except your travel, you could be auditioned for and participate in films which gave students the chance of having experienced actors to film alongside people of less ability and experience. I remember doing films in particular for the LCP, the London College of Printing. Dominic Gros' film called 'Lulu' with a screen adaptation of the Lulu story – a young girl rejects the fervent advances of her teacher (played by Emil Jannings in the film). This won the Fuji Prize and was thought to be good enough to precede the latest film by Jean Luc Godard at the National Film Theatre which was really quite an honour so it wasn't necessarily a low standard (the script was by Maggie Brookes for instance) it was just slow working with inexperienced people.

I made a film for the National Film School and the Royal College of Art, all of which won these prizes and launched the student directors into their careers.

I trained and examined other guides as part of my work as a guide and was accepted as a Fellow of the Guild of Guide Lecturers – I think I was number 15 to be so rewarded out of a role of about 650 so it was a sought after and prestigious thing to happen.

I was accepted into the Art Historians' Association, largely at the instigation of the University of London and had some excellent reviews of my other work. I gave a public lecture called "Breaking New Ground" at the National Gallery in front of the actual paintings which prompted the Director to ask me to talk at the Gallery about anything at any time – rare praise indeed. Equally, I gave a lecture in French on the State of Modern Art, Contemporary Art if you like at The Museum of Modern Art in Calais which was very well attended and the Director was delighted that I went to the heart of the matter without getting lost in the peripheries of art history, connoisseurship etc.

I wrote and presented a piece for the World Service of the BBC about Speaking English which a friend of mine who was filming in Africa heard – it was broadcast pretty well all over the known world.

So I guess in this way I was putting back.

The other non-career jobs : postman x 2, bus conductor x 2 and encyclopaedia type salesman etc. were done when I was a student at Glasgow.

CHAPTER 9

STUDENT – COURTAULD INSTITUTE OF ART.

The typical Courtauld student was a wee bit precious but not necessarily all by any means and our gang consisted of what has become several professors and so on. We used to joke around and have drinks at midday and so on – clown around a bit generally. So that's not so bad. I do remember however one of the girls – a buxom harridan – complaining on a Monday morning that 'Starlight had thrown her and she was aching all over' to which one of our gang of rather proletarian provenance replied 'Have you had it on an ironing board?' So that's the way it was. But two very stimulating years.

The same applies... we went for a little course on the physicality of painting, the technology of painting and so on and I remember the lecturer saying, 'Always apply two fat luscious layers of paint before you begin,' and I said to the rather well brought up lady next to me, 'Sounds like the Kama Sutra, doesn't it?' She furrowed her brow for a bit and then said, 'I don't know,' I said, 'Do you know the Kama Sutra? And she said, 'I don't know, where is it?' What you might call the great divide.

However, it was pleasant enough all in all. We did some live visits such as Guildford Cathedral, the 'Spencer' Memorial

Chapel, the paintings at Royal Holloway College. We were taken en masse to see the Marat Sade with Glenda Jackson in it and afterwards discussed it from a literary point of view with the professor of French. We had lectures by the like of Kenneth Clarke and Nikolaus Pevsner who also gave us tutorials on British Architecture. We were tutored by Pevsner, Rainer Banham, John Golding, Anita Brookner, Phoebe Poole and so on.

An afterthought: it was the first year I believe of the 'special subject' forming part of the final exam. I chose Michelangelo to whom I was highly responsive, the result being that the Director of the Victoria and Albert Museum, who was my assessor, was very pleased with what I did.

It was all top of the range you could say – a most worthwhile two years postgraduate study and it brought me up to date. Thank goodness because as soon as I finished, I went to work at an art school with very contemporary painters and students practising a whole range of skills. I was Director of History of Art and Complementary Studies at the West Sussex College of Art, Worthing, an interview that I'd had during term time – in other words I already had a job to go to when I finished at the Courtauld so it was a great and again seamless transition. And this time there was no football involved! …until a little later … and then there was!

CHAPTER 10

HEAD OF DEPARTMENT – WEST SUSSEX COLLEGE OF ART.

We were living in Shepherds Bush at the time and we set off one morning in great state in HUMPHREY as we called him which was a 1947 Morris 8 as I recall and we'd been to Rome in it, would you believe – top speed 45mph so we went up the Alps rather leisurely and down the Alps rather speedily I seem to remember but we got there with a 45ft turning circle. Three weeks it took us there and back and it came back and just sort of went 'pughghgh'.

Anyway in this car we went to see, as near as we could, where we would live. The job itself was in Worthing which we went through without quite noticing we had reached our destination and continued along the Brighton Road to something that really appealed to us. We finished up probably in the highest set accommodation in the town which was right at the top of the hill which goes from the station as a third of a kind of villa with three families in it. It was spacious and delightful except – there's always an except isn't there – except for people animatedly discussing shall we say boisterously late at night at one end of the ground floor and people clumping about at the other end first thing in the morning. We were above them both on the first floor so we got the noise of goodnight protracted discussions shall we say – heated usually – on the ground floor

– and then 7 o'clock in the morning at the latest we got, 'Hello, hello the sun's here,' from the other end so where we lived on the first floor was a bit problematic but, for a time, it was very nice indeed thank you very much with the tiniest glimpse of the sea but nevertheless a glimpse and, as it seemed, infinite space.

We formed a circle which included Dave and Dilys Foster (painters), Robert Simmonds (film maker), Jeff Keane (multifarious artist) Colin Hadley (caricaturist), Annie Hadley (costume designer/cutter), Dave Ward (ceramic sculptor), Ronnie Ward (fashion designer) Ned Hoskins (designer).

It all seems a brave new world but we did see the 1966 World Cup in our place in Brighton which coincided with a delivery of wine from France. Fergus Roy, a student mate from Glasgow and his wonderful black Labrador Mickey were our guests on this day. All we need to do now is to find ships to go into the empty bottles.

The job was mostly sharing enthusiasm for what I had acquired a taste for-environmental things, poetry, street theatre and the history of art generally I suppose and initiatives that were stirring in the early sixties, not least in Brighton itself with its festival and so on. It was s passionate discovery and sharing the enthusiasm I felt for these things with the students so it rather romped along. I remember the Principal asked me to organise a kind of 'away day' for the entire staff and student body, the entire college which was a tremendous idea and great fun to do. We had a staff vs students football match – aah, 'played for the local football team!' I played in goal in an improvised sort of way until it was 8 or 9 nil and the students drove a Land Rover across the goal to declare a truce, the whole shebang refereed by the model, Muriel. We then had a showing of 'Some Like it Hot' which had been out for a little while. I had already started a film society there so that was all set up with a projector separated from the auditorium by two layers of for certain see-through glass and so on. It was quite nice conditions to see a film in the lecture hall and on a flat surface so that it wasn't canted towards one end. Then we put on a play or rather the last rehearsal of a play i.e. we all read from a script – a little play I had written in pantomime form about a fairground called "King Leer" and half the staff were in it, as you would expect. It went down rather well – it was all just jolly. In the evening we had a fancy dress ball and Maggie took away the first prize – a bottle of Chanel No 5 for dressing as a negress which was uncommon in that part of the world but she did find one of her pupils ethnic enough to dress her up properly and she had to go in next day to her posh English school with black stains everywhere. Anyway it was good fun and we finished off the day with jacket potatoes in the embers of the fire on a steel plate in the car park. I think we can honestly say 'a good time was had by all' and a tremendously significant and delightful initiative by the college. The next year the theme of the fancy dress was – the army – military so Maggie and I went as Salvation Army personnel – drab but quite enterprising...no prizes. It's the idea isn't it? I also started a college magazine, we had an exhibition open to the public for the first time, a students union for the first time and bought a monstrous order of library books (brand new) for a newly established library, (including the furniture) and crowned in a glass case by the Jeff Keene Pilot in a DC 3 Seat which, since his sad death, must be worth a helluva lot. One or two leaders of disciplines were given 25 quid each for various things for example the bloke in Graphics bought a Lawrence Cutting print – again a nice idea – a college or principal's initiative – all these things made for a companionable atmosphere. So especially the first year when it was all brand new to me, it was pretty fantastic. The second year was still consolidation but it was a bit more difficult – the impetus of total discovery and innovation wasn't there but nevertheless, it was the same "firm" and a thoroughly worthwhile couple of years.

The Principal wanted to take me to Canada with him to where he was changing his job to a university there but I told him that my future as I saw it was in London so that was graciously passed over. So I found myself without this marvellous income which finished up largely in the restaurants of Brighton and abroad and a succession of cars – I got as far as a Renault 8 by the time I left there and pitched myself on London as did Maggie. She worked in a polytechnic – that was her step up and I was able eventually to get into 5 different things including the Open University and the extension service of the University of London doing art history mostly but the openhearted enterprising curriculum of the Open University foundation arts course was expansive, then Renaissance and Reformation and Renaissance and Modern Period of the University of London – that lasted me till 1973/4 and, by then, I had the acting bug catch me unawares on the latter days of our stay in Brighton, it was nibbling away at me – more of this, as we change the scene again.

There's a certain amount of rocking and rolling in this tale I'm sure you realise – time shifts as I remember things. I hope I am forgiven.

CHAPTER 11

ODD JOBS AND MORE ART SCHOOLS.

Because I had resigned from my job I was told I was not entitled to unemployment benefits or possibly even to sign on for a job. There was a rather splendid north country bloke there at the time listening in to all the booths and he said he was looking for labourers to set up an exhibition in the town, in Brighton and would I like to do that and the answer was, 'Yes of course I would like to be an exhibition designer's labourer and set up an exhibition in Brighton'. In the meantime I had done copy ironically for one of the exhibitors who was selling artificial eyelashes so I did this labouring job wearing my father's army boots I think. I went to see my handiwork at the exhibition itself which was a bit of a shock for the higher-ups of the exhibition scene but not so much for my mates – the exhibition design mates. All rather ironic but at the time, it saved the day.

The hunt was then on to find a job in London.

I had been working at Guildford School of Art from the previous September and was fitting in there rather well – had some good mates and found the students interesting and then the bombshell hit – 1968. I can honestly say I'm still a bit baffled as to what it was all about since I was a brand newcomer. The acid test was: "Are you 100% for the status quo or do you 100% reject the status quo?" – from the Vice Principal whom I had never seen before. This was the first time I had heard of this – so there was no room for meaningful debate of any kind. I objected to this on principle which seemed to put me on the side of the "villains" and we got this writ to forbid us to go onto the premises and so on. So I began in earnest to move to London and seek out a job. I think the first thing I did was to be accepted by the University of London as Extension Lecturer in the History of Art. I remember going to my first class and getting a phone call from my Head of Dept. at Guildford imploring me to join him and his colleagues in a sit-in at Guildford which I didn't subscribe to. I had already attended a general meeting and explained that some are more engaged than others in the politics and that I wanted to teach above all and moreover there might have been some students that wanted to learn above all.

I must confess I'm still a bit baffled by the ins and outs. Anyway, I asked at my union (they had to form a branch especially, the ATTI at Guildford) what should be done and they said, 'keep out of it,' basically so I cobbled together a continued career as an art history lecturer.

I also decided I would go and train in the discus and shot at Tooting Bec Athletic Ground which was used for The Chariots of Fire I discovered later and tried to improve on my distances and times and finished up throwing the discus for Herne Hill Harriers whose ground I was training on – not bad after a 10 year gap (this was when we were living in Streatham). A lovely shower and Chinese meal on the way back after the task. I made the most of it although it was a very brow-furrowing time.

I survived it alright but not without difficulty. I added the Open University and subsequently 3 rather prestigious Art Schools – I was determined to return to work I suppose having been so lightly dismissed from Guilford. It became a bit hairless trying to mix and match all the commitments I'd set myself up for but for a time it worked rather well and was interesting – new material, new people. I remember one or two highlights:

At Croydon I got theatre students to perform, in a rudimentary way, from Chaucer which I'd translated – the technician took photographs of the whole sequence of performance. That was extremely worth doing and at Walthamstow I collaborated – very kindly on his part, with Keith Albarn on sites, empty sites we'd discovered in Walthamstow and we had the benefit of his critique, his expertise with that. It was a general atmosphere of 'getting on with it'. It really was thrusting, the ideas that students came up with.

One particular moment should be sung about – as a special treat I was given a group of better-than-art-school-dressed plumbing students. After a lot of thought, I presented to them a miscellany of slides and asked them what would be an appropriate title.

The bulls eye came when we were looking at "Bronze Loop" I think by Annesley and the class genius came out with 'Lesbian' – there was a frisson bigger than Pinter – as he explained, "Bent bit of brass ain'it?" A Treasure. This was at Hammersmith College of Art and Building. A wide spectrum of students and I started work on an adult playground for the Yucca Plantation in Holland Park until insurance difficulties stopped it.

I remember on the other side contributing a criticism of 'That'll Be the Day' for the first number of a magazine we were trying to get together – so we were pushing the envelope a bit.

CHAPTER 12

TUTOR TO THE UNIVERSITY OF LONDON, THE OPEN UNIVERSITY, MAGIC CARPET.

Alongside all this is my film artistes and acting career.

I taught for the Open University for 3 years and for the closed, as I used to jokingly call it – the University Extension for 6 years. When I went to the Deputy Director of the university extension (or some high heed yin) and asked if I could take a year off doing courses for them, to be in a play – I never got a chance to explain it was Paul Daneman and Dorothy Tutin in Macbeth, directed by Peter Coe, he got red behind the ears – he clearly did not like his administration perturbed. Anyway, the long and the short of it was he reluctantly took it as final rather than agreed, and pointed out I would have great difficulty in applying again afterwards. We never discussed the merits of the project itself although I believe he had a literary background. Anyway, it was rather sad and I was somewhat disappointed. It led to a kind of malaise which resulted in me taking a chance by talking to the vice principal at Croydon about this year off and he thought this was a good idea. How much further it went, I don't know – I was still a bit wet behind the ears. At

Walthamstow they were a bit upset that I had done this (I'd resigned from Walthamstow). It was a bit more traumatic than it need have been. What I should have done was waited one more year to set it up before I took this year off and see how things went and it was meant to be a year off. I'd get new material, new experiences, new things to do. I would come back after a year with a tale to tell.

So I was left with the beginnings of a guide course a bit of acting stuff and working on Magic Carpet productions with pretty high optimism but the income and success generally did rather go down after that sort of date which was 74 or so. I was in my play of Macbeth I believe at that date. This was to play Lennox who was quite intimately involved with the plot so a good thing to do in a Number One national tour with Peter Coe who directed the Hamlet I mentioned at the Globe Theatre Bankside so I got to see all these places here and there round England and took the opportunity when I wasn't actually performing to get material for An Invitation to England so there were some nice shots of York and Stoke-on-Trent etc which eventually turned up in An Invitation to England. I always seem to want to do something else when I'm doing something. When I was doing the acting tours I was always working on the videos at the same time. It worked well enough, better than slouching round the same dotted line in the town or getting sloshed.

I was touting Magic Carpet Productions myself with reasonable success. Nearly everybody I approached accepted an initial order I must say (a notable exception being Cambridge University Central Library – 'A video!? But we haven't finished cataloguing the Incunabula!') and I was very proud of that but I got obsessed and felt I had to do it – put notches on the bedpost so to speak – and it was a lot of wear and tear – a bit neurotic on my part. A good idea but I should have left it alone, having set it up.

CHAPTER 13

THE BEGINNINGS OF SHOWBIZ.

I've skated over "A Moment of Revelation on a Mountain Top."
   There I was at the pinnacle of Brighton, gazing out to sea enjoying my job at the Art School well enough and having this idea – Richard Attenborough was filming 'Oh What a Lovely War' at the end of Brighton Pier – and I thought, 'I'd like to be in that,' so I sauntered down the hill to the pier and went to the end, well prepared to stand around and join in to start with of course in this marvellous film. Well, talk about naïve! I was greeted with a crescendo of 'Union, union, union, union!' As I made overtures to the various personnel, I got the message eventually and, with as much dignity as I could muster, went back off the pier and subsequently, as advised, went with a five pound note prominently to the fore, to the Film Artistes Association in London and registered as a film extra. I was very lucky. I was 6'2" with a flowing red beard and weighed about 16st I would say at that time and I found reasonable success with roles in, especially, 'Elizabethan' films. Polanski 'Big Peter – you come here and stand in the middle.' Off I went to be a royal thane in the Macbeth with Francesca Annis and Jon Finch. Fantastic to be that near real acting. To cut a long story short, the Hitchcock film Frenzy had me as a newspaper reading 'passerby'. So effective was I that I couldn't be – without being recognised – a Covent Garden porter in the afternoon, said Alfred Hitchcock, so

*Royal Thane attending Lady Macbeth (Francesca Annis)
in the banquet scene (directed by Polanski).*

I was put in charge of the extras' clothes (ordinary clothes).

I talked to a casting director subsequently about this and he said, 'Don't be an extra that can speak lines,' so I started again with Equity membership, Spotlight, agents, adverts and so on and gently worked my way through until I got better and better parts as I became better and better known – considerable improvement. I finished up doing Peter Coe Productions in the theatre like Hamlet which opened the Globe Theatre Bankside and then Macbeth with Paul Daneman, Dotty Tutin, Gary Raymond and so on which went on a brief tour starting at Guildford. I did national tours of The Ghost Train directed by Roger Redfarn and a play about Churchill directed by Mr. Bentall as we think of him – a very dignified old school director – Michael Bentall with Nigel Stock playing Churchill, Barbara Jefford playing Lady Churchill. I understudied Nigel Stock's Churchill which was a great experience. We really collaborated on the research for it over pints of Guinness. One was learning not to be naïve. That was a lovely experience. I never went on for him but I went through the motions and rehearsed as an understudy for the role – very fulfilling indeed (A Man and His Wife). So I got that far really.

I remember Glenda Jackson made several films – I was lurking about in the Music Lovers with Richard Chamberlain and then became her stage manager in The Incredible Sarah with a galaxy of stars – and that was a promotion. I went to see Richard Fleischer for a part as a furniture removal man and stared him in the face when I was answering questions and he said, 'This is not a staring competition Mr. Davidson,' I said, 'I'm sure you want to see my reactions and I'm interested to show them to you,' so stage manager – wonderful. That promotion pleased me. Equally, to be understudying Churchill pleased me. And to be taken out of a large

With Glenda Jackson and Daniel Massey in a scene from 'The Incredible Sarah'. Directed by Richard Fleischer.

cast of soldiers to play the Second Gravedigger to Ron Moody's First Gravedigger – a promotion which was nice. And I was asked several times by directors I had worked for to do something else for them which I applaud and am proud of – why not?

So this career went that way. I started as a film extra and became a fairly sought-after speaker in productions. I think the most exciting thing I did was to create the part of the King in The Pixie Led at the Latchmere Theatre – Christopher Harris's play where I was the first actor to touch this part which later transferred to America so that was all discovery and very very fulfilling indeed – the King in The Pixie Led. Roughly at the same time, I played Samuel Randall, the Liverpool slave trader, in 'Indigo' by Heidi Thomas at the Almeida so things were beginning to bubble along together really.

There was a lot of television and quite a bit of film and radio plays for the 3rd programme as it was – radio 3 I think directed by Piers Plowright, Walter Dacosta and Vanessa Whitburn. Precious Bane with Miriam Margolyes – all these very worthy and enjoyable to do.

I did a lot of Plays for Today for television, including Donal and Sally about a sort of Romeo and Juliet couple with learning difficulties with Sylvestra Le Touzel and Gerard Kelly (I played the Gardiner) and Billy, about a fight between Social Services and a family, Lost Hole in Babylon about the Spaghetti House siege. I guess that strain took me to play the sergeant with Anthony Hopkins in the remake in colour of Great Expectations which was a kind of kudos part to get.

So that was how it was going but sadly had to stop because of ill-health.

I honestly can say that I've lost count of how many characters I've played one way and another between commercials and radio, television, cinema and theatre but that's something to be proud of.

My CV includes the legendary Willie Baxter, the hero of the Scott's Porage Oats Adverts, legendary because Benny Hill did a

spoof version of it and I hope he enjoyed it as much as I did –
'Och now' – this was a heavily bearded middle-aged grocer in a
bashful love affair with a feisty woman, called Mrs Monroe. We
did 3 commercials for TV – at the time of the second one, I'd been
playing the executioner in St.Joan for Jane Howell so had no beard.
However, the sound man's chest hair fitted the bill perfectly so that
was harvested until he got fed up. We just made it.

There was also a radio commercial with 'Willie'. Nell
Brennan (Mrs Monroe) was doing a play in Ireland so we met
at the Eamon Andrews Studios in Dublin.

But I achieved a bit of celebrity with the man in the street on
account of all that. I'm still not sure whether it was a good thing
but my father even introduced me to a stranger as "Willie Baxter"!

So there you are – so much for the glamour of showbusiness
and meanwhile the drums are beating in the jungle. Maggie, who
had been a courier, had applied for the London Tourist Board
Blue Badge Guide course and I got more and more interested in
that and finally went for the interview, passed and signed up.

Trial Scene from St. Joan (with Gabrielle Lloyd), directed by Jane Howell.

CHAPTER 14

SHOW ME THE WAY TO GO HOME – TOURIST GUIDING!

A London Tourist Board Blue Badge guide is not an easy thing to be. Many of the guides are graduates and they come from pretty well all over the world, although the course itself is given in English. There's so much involved in this, I'll try and sketch it out so that there's a bit of colour in it without being too precise about everything. We had lectures in County Hall on Thursday night for 2 hours. We did live trips on a Saturday, normally taking the whole day. We did trips to visit various sites, including museums and we were set essays encompassing knowledge of all these things and they were very serious about the logistics of it – crowd control is a crucial ingredient. If you showed weak crowd control, as you demonstrated Rembrandt's development in the National Gallery, you would risk failing the course entirely. So it was meticulous in its demands. Although I'd been to 2 universities, the volume of the facts and the variety of the skills you had to learn was almost daunting. I must say both Maggie and I felt diffident at our chances of passing the exam but at the last minute girded our loins and went through the process with success and indeed enjoyed guiding mostly very much. The course lasted 6 months and was quite expensive

I may say and pretty well full time by the time you had done, research, thought about your essays and done all the reading required etc. Among the skills you learn is guiding people backwards, facing the people in the coach with your back to the driver i.e. to where you're going and telling them – sometimes in three languages, what they're about to see, where they're about to see it, from that position which is left and right, as far as they're concerned and the opposite to you really is quite difficult but once you've got it, you've got it. Thereafter you have a bit of a passe-partout. You tend to swan into posh hotels and ask for tariffs with your blue badge blazing away on your lapel. You are of course allowed to enter Westminster Abbey, St Paul's and various places you would normally pay with the showing of this blue badge to say nothing of Parliament where I and a lot of other people guided visitors around as well as the things already mentioned so it's various apart from anything else.

Anywhere you can reach in a day and back again from London is the fundamental structure. It might be Canterbury, it might be Stratford-upon-Avon. It might be Stonehenge, it might be Dover. Round Britain tours are also done and some people take parties abroad as well. So it's quite a rich profession actually and there's a lot to it.

I did have the idea of asking Chris Searle to spend a day as a tourist guide – you remember he was an opera singer and various other things for a day on TV to show how the preparation was done. It still remains a good idea but I couldn't honestly deal with it myself at the time and there wasn't any immediate pick up from anybody else. I think the general public once they've been on a tour, understand but, until they do, they don't realise how much they can get from a guide and how sophisticated guides can be.

At first, turning the theoretical into the practical is very difficult.

My first tour was supposed to be to Windsor but we landed at Terminal 3, Heathrow Airport – most people didn't realise the Queen lives with her family at Heathrow! "Heathrow Castle".

I was eventually elected as a Fellow of the Guild of Guide Lecturers – it's a helluva long way from my Heathrow wobbly to a FGGL!

So I worked for several companies but two companies in particular who took you on 'dry runs' and did all they could to prepare you on the road as it were and then went freelance as I've said. The work included French sommeliers, French firemen, French members of parliament which I did in French of course but also salesmen on incentive tours from all sorts of places ,cabinet makers from Switzerland on a tour of The London College of Furniture etc. The variety is pretty immense. The trip with the sommeliers round the House of Lords was one of the nicest things I remember – I remember George Thomas – the famous Torriepandy Welshman who was Speaker – came up to us and asked who we were. I explained it was a French group and he said 'Ah! Liberty, Equality and Brotherhood' – and we were of course in the House of Lords – he was the Speaker of the House of Commons – so he declared, 'You're in the wrong place boyo!' which was a lovely point of contact and shows how the work can be at its best. To cap it all, it was on my return from this tour, that I found a bottle of champagne outside my flat door. As I keep saying about other things, it was companionable. There was a separate course for the Palace of Westminster – really quite long and arduous. You had to learn all the safety procedures as much as the history. But it's amazing when on television you see The State Opening of Parliament for example, there is this tremendous recognition as they go through The Ceremony. Genuine knowledge and insights come into it – how else would you get inside Smithfield Meat Market? You're privy to a lot of, well, closely guarded ideas such as The Livery Companies – yes you're taken in almost as a colleague by such institutions and it's a nice feeling.

There's a lot of agony and ecstasy involved – for instance finding yourself running round the Changing of the Guard trying to find a missing member of your group is one of the unpleasant sides to it.

One of the nicest things that happened to me I must tell you is ; we went on a tour to Stratford and left in a bit of a hurry – hustle and bustle – and it was only at Oxford that I remembered to introduce myself and said, 'Oh, ladies and gentlemen, my name is Peter by the way,' and we carried on to Warwick etc. It was at the end of the tour as the tourists went back to their hotel, one chap came up to me and said 'Great tour Mr. Bytheway!' Marvellous! I had hot dinners on that for quite a long time. A good job – various, not all pleasant but when it works, it's terrific.

In 1983, at the time of the Gulf War, I had a viral infection which put me in hospital for 5 weeks where I was dialyzed and so on – it really was a pretty harrowing time for everybody involved and I came out very grateful indeed for the expertise of King's College Hospital, I was feeling a bit of a wet rag I must confess and I decided to push forward with something I'd started a little before which was to make a video (which it was then) of London – An Invitation to London which was tape and slides primarily and took a visitor or impending visitor on a tour of London as a tape slide show and it was received with tremendous acclaim by the Editor of the London Evening Standard who wrote a glowing article in praise of it – I was obviously very pleased indeed with this. I did that just before the hospital visit and I'd done a couple of stories on tape as well for my godchildren and so I began to embark on Magic Carpet Productions – audiovisual presentations beginning with An Invitation to London transferred from tape-slide, tape calibrated for slide changes – each time a slide came, the tape signalled to a machine so the commentary would follow very well in unison. I transferred that whole thing onto videotape which was the coming thing with a bank loan of £10,000, basically unsecured which cost me in the end 75% interest – I paid seventeen and half thousand pounds back – so I won't name my sponsor – you can guess. The period of payback took a long time obviously but it was finally done. It did pay for itself and I'm pleased to say it went all over the world to libraries and schools and so on and in this country again to libraries,individuals, art schools and was sold by just about everybody from Harrods to the National English Library at Euston. I sold spoken word cassettes of my readings of the big poets like Coleridge, John Donne, Thomas Hardy and so on to places like HMV and Virgin – at the time just about blanket coverage of all outlets which made me a bit hairless I must confess, traipsing round London, asking if they'd sold any and replacing them if they had. But it was a use of the imagination and I must say that because everything paid for itself it wasn't vanity publishing. More than this, because of An Invitation to London, I was asked to make a video about Russia by a company that took pupils – from the age of 16 onwards – to the Soviet Union as it then was. So I did. I accompanied a school, at various seasons of the year, from Peterborough I think. Off we went and did it all from their point of view. It had been made before with Richard Baker – I suspect rather more objectively and they wanted an update so I took their part and joined in, which was successful.

Lines of communication were very sophisticated: we were

ferried around in once-upon-a-time sleek black limousines. I had an interpreter from Intourist who translated my instructions into Russian for Mikael Levine, a Department of Information cameraman. After a while we went round without an interpreter because it soon became clear that Mikael's assent to a technical request was "Bing Crosby" whereas inspirations were greeted with a jubilant, "Elvis Presley"!

We scored a bullseye for Anglo-Soviet understanding with our picnic on the overnight train from St Petersburg to Moscow – his vodka and my chocolate Easter eggs. 'Horrasha!'★

★All these Russian experiences were at the time of the Presidency of Mikael Gorbachev – before the fall of the Berlin Wall. The objective is to present the pageant of Russia as it was at the time rather than wider political issues.

I asked if I could sell the video commercially if I paid them a royalty which they accepted so it joined the other titles including my own poetry. There's a total of 50 titles at least between videos, cassettes and CDs and the proudest thing I believe is An Invitation to Contemporary Art which draws naturally on my training and experience generally over a long period of teaching in art schools etc. That has been sold at Tate Modern for over 20 years – sold successfully and consistently re-ordered so I'm obviously very pleased. There are various fringe benefits that go with having four and a half careers and doing a lot of odd jobs. I was very pleased to take Maggie to the Soviet Union to be there when the Invitation to Russia was being made and explore on her own behalf. She took me along on a visit to the United States on the invitation of a group of tourists that she had taken on a coach trip. Both journeys widened and it sharpened our capacity for surprise. One was almost on the crest of the dunes in the crosswind being amazed by aeroplanes filling the sky.

CHAPTER 15

NAME CHANGE AND THEATRE.

In the meantime, we've had a "complete change of costume":

I was doing an episode of All Creatures Great and Small up in Yorkshire with Peter Davison and a cast including Robert Hardy and it emerged that Peter was about to play Doctor Who and our names were very similar so an agent could easily get the wrong one. For a while I had been getting enquiries for the young lothario parts and he was getting enquiries for the grandfather on the Russian throne or such a thing. Since I was a member of Equity before Peter Davison, I could have dug my heels in but I let him keep Peter Davison and decided after a session at the Acton Hilton, the BBC rehearsal rooms in North London, about 2.30 in the afternoon people like Windsor Davis helped me decide. We had a pint or two and a game of pool and sat in the sunshine in plenary session and tossed around the idea of an alternative. In the end we came up with PJ Davidson. John is my middle name and I remember in secondary school signing PJ Davidson so that was the conclusion. It was a bit ironic because Peter Davison had chosen that name because his own was similar to an existing member and he chose Peter Davison without checking and the similarity only came out when I pointed it out. Equity accepted the difference of course and, acknowledging it was their fault, a free advert was put in the Stage, saying that I was now P J Davidson.

The idea was that Orson Welles might say, "We'll shoot the next scene in Paris if that's ok with PJ." One can dream!

I was in an episode of The Professionals and my job was to be a lorry driver, thoroughly fed up sitting in a traffic jam, the length of the motorway pretty well. The lorry itself was about as long as the Palace of Westminster, 16 gears it had. It also had a mate, a driver's mate called James MacManus. Well we did the usual English things, counted the buttons on our shirts, stared at the embankments on either side to see if they had built a new town there by now and generally whiled away the time and fell to talking which became more and more enjoyable and more and more revelatory and it seemed we had an enormous amount in common so duly arranged to meet up again in 'civvy street' and I remember visiting his garden/parties quite frequently with other luminaries, then going to see shows at the Music Hall where he was Chairman from time to time, saw him in the panto at the Stratford East Theatre. Also went to see him play Hancock brilliantly in 'Hancock's Last Half Hour' at The New End Theatre in Hampstead.

Anyway, he was at one of our shindigs with some other worthies and we realised we'd have to look for some wine one way or another but instead we had the idea of the phy*kit club. Its manifesto was really to subvert the serious and the orderly in life, i.e.conformity. We began with the boules which we played quite frequently on the Terrace overlooking the gardens and down to the River so instead of the extensive rules published in French, it was more a question of:

When throwing the ball, you must have both feet in the same county – and things of that kind and there were various manifesto rules. The founder members were Maggie Davidson,

Peter Davidson, Colin Hadley, the illustrator Annie Hadley, the costume designer/cutter David Foster and Dilys Foster (painters) and Banquo probably. There was one Extraordinary Meeting of the club chez nous and we'd had enough of subverting for a bit so we settled down to a very formal discussion about policy with things like 'Minutes of the last Meeting', 'Agenda' etc. 'punishment for somebody wearing a tie' and so on – all very meticulous. It almost became serious. Around that point, Jim Macmanus, who had set this up about half an hour before had got out onto the balcony, closed the window behind him unnoticed and now mimed trying to get in – it seemed to go on for ten minutes. Anyway, he was admitted as an extraordinary member and business continued as usual. You can see where we were at. We felt we'd been serious enough, all of us and met up occasionally to have these highly productive meetings, don't ye know! Fortunately I have retained a childlike sense of awe and surprise, there was even an occasional outburst of infantility. For instance, we went to an exhibition snooker evening with Ray Reardon in Somerset. He was really very good, if a little formal. Anyway, he leant over the table – miles across it – took a spider to do one of the shots and, absolutely bang on cue, somebody farted (I'm laughing now) in the front row. 3 people laughed – me and 2 others – that's why we founded the ---t club !

The ball I threw into the air as a child has not yet reached the ground!

'Indigo' by Heidi Thomas was put on at the Almeida in a very timely way because the whole nation was pretty well focussed particularly on the anniversary of the abolition of the slave trade whose hub had been Liverpool. I played Samuel Randall, a Liverpool slave trader and the continuous vindictive attitude to my son is paralleled by that of an African Chief and

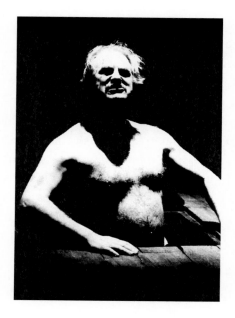

Samuel Randall in 'Indigo' by Heidi Thomas (directed by Keith Boak).

his son. They never meet dramatically. It's very poetic in many ways, very moving indeed and is just one expression of that consciousness of the evils of the Slave Trade. Maggie Hambling made a sculpture out of abandoned chains on The Liverpool Dock, for instance.★

This play was recommended for the Evening Standard Drama Award by Milton Schulman which was rare praise. He singled out, apart from the important subject, the poetry of the piece. Heidi Thomas has gone on to make quite a name for herself in television drama in particular.

'The Pixie Led' by Christopher Harris was very much its first production of all at the Latchmere Theatre so when I came to play my part – "the King" – it had never been done before. It was absolutely virgin territory and an enormous sense of responsibility, I might add. The play is about a whore, a clerk and the "king" who have been incarcerated by the regime. The sort of curtain raiser for this is Gogol and I suppose the piece is unmistakably Russian in its feeling and Gogolesque in its manner of production. Every time we are persecuted – the clerk, the whore and me, who are together – break out into fantasy, wishful thinking and a kind of charade which is all the more poignant for having to return to the banalities and realities of our incarceration. It's a solemn piece which went to America just after our production at the Latchmere. It's very funny and very moving. Not long after that, there was a production in South East London(Southwark Playhouse) – very much within living memory – which I was invited to see naturally. It was totally different. While we had a ruined, messed up, kind of stable interior as a set (we were in prison remember), they had cuboid shapes covered in red, carefully ironed fabric so, to that extent, abstractly set which obviously had a different intention from the realism which ran through our production. One of the things that interested me was, there was a notorious speech (I'm not going to give away jokes – he's not only the king) in which he compares Spain and China in an absolutely loony way which is really euphoric in many ways – very funny, very quicksilver speaking and very intricately written, similar to what you find sometimes in Ionesco. We had such a short rehearsal period that I never managed to get that off pat, I must say. So short was it that none of us in the cast had looked at the 4th act before we did this rehearsed reading (Stage Directions read by Sylvia Sims) as a preview for VIPs' – other actors. The production in South East London had the Spain/China speech in its entirety – which distinguishes it from our earlier ground-breaking production.

*I recently was told that more slaves died in transit than died in the Holocaust.

*Dress rehearsal shots from 'The Pixie Led', by Christopher Harris
(with Nigel Betts) directed by Julian Richards*

Actors usually vouchsafe their attitude to reviews don't they, so I wouldn't want to break that tradition. I've had not all that many reviews because the things I've done have not been stardom by any means, with one or two exceptions. I have climbed Mount Olympus and I hope other actors are listening to this – I've achieved nirvana by having a good review in The Stage which was: 'Peter Davidson's performance exerts a fascination. 'This was for The King or about the King.'

The one I value in that regard is – 'occasionally the ensemble playing attains majesty' which I thought was a wonderful tribute to the way the whore, the clerk and the king tried to put over something in the end very sensitive – so that was a very rewarding review as far as we were concerned. The sort of "review" if you like that I value is comments from authors whose work I've played on the stage or wherever, from the likes of Trevor Griffiths or Peter MacDougal. Peter did the wonderful Play for Today called Donal and Sally and promised me a lifetime of parts playing 'the polis'. For Trevor Griffiths I played in Bill Brand with everybody – Jack Shepherd, Arthur Lowe, Geoffrey Palmer, Rosemary Martin, George Wearing, to say nothing of Alan Badel. And also for Trevor, Sons and Lovers in which I played Mr. Leivers, the girl's father – both directed by Stuart Burge. It's always complimentary to work again for a director which has happened to me several times. It really gives you a pat on the back and enormous confidence and ease when you play another role for this particular individual. This has happened particularly with Richard Bramall and Jane Howell as well. This is why the letter I is supposed to be the most worn character on the typewriter belonging to an actor who " told the tale". I'm very aware of this. I could of course fabricate things by talking about 'we' and 'one' – that would be hysterical.

CHAPTER 16

ONE AND ONLY COMPANY.

We had good relations with the College of Dramatic Art when we were at Glasgow and I should mention that we had a very strong connection with Grace Matchett, a member of the staff there who directed plays for us (it was very good of the University to pay for a professional director.

She was an inspiration. Among the best known and well loved aphorisms a whole generation of students will treasure will be Grace saying, 'Mr. Seymour-Jones, I've been looking at your costume and do you know what it looks like? It looks like a pig's arse!' I still laugh at this because he was very self regarding and a little bit pompous for his age and Grace was just being matter of fact really, but wow!

During this time at Glasgow there was a student play competition won by Anne Garside – Johan Dory it was called and on the judging panel was also the Principal of the Drama College and a representative of the Dramatic Society as well. It was a very vivid play about an undertaker and to make the point it was a student's play, as well as funny, we processed around the whole University area of Glasgow with a coffin – a mock kind of funeral with Pat who played football in the same team as me (a Catholic priest) purporting to conduct the service, handing out leaflets saying, 'Come and see this at the students' union' which we did, temporarily interrupted when a whole procession of people beginning at the top and slowly going down to the ground, left the auditorium during the actual performance saying, "Leave the Pope alone"…repeatedly. It was a pretty innocuous statement. It was set in hell and the Pope says, 'Come to Hell for Happy Holy Days!' Anyway a whole row just got up and walked out.

I'm reminded of it in Alan Franks' play 'Our Boys' (Falklands War) There's a moment of complete contempt for Margaret Thatcher – I was about to say 'who was on the throne but who was Prime Minister at the time. The subject of the play was the Falklands conflict and you could feel the rugby playing audience inching psychologically towards the stage in disgruntlement. It was in a room above a pub so they were on the same level fundamentally as we were and all we could really do sensibly was to play the play that much harder and we did and we won but talk about electricity in the theatre! But that's live theatre for you.

We've been nudging towards "Do It Yourself Theatre", so I might as well confess to the ultimate in this genre:

One balmy summer evening, the mob, a gang of us – the chatting classes, found ourselves in the local deli being congenial. It was the sort of evening where the air was made minestrone soup by the mosquitoes. It was the sort of evening where there was room for nothing but apathy. We ran out of ideas for discussion on the merits of goat's cheese compared to Wensleydale and slowly turned to our favourite plays and were astonished to see that most people thought that The Importance of Being Earnest was the greatest thing. We were in that kind of mood.

Well… it was a tiny step from that to 'Let's put it on – but with a difference – and before you could say 'Laurence Olivier, there we were with a map of the set which we decided would

The One and Only Company (versus Stanislavski!) in
'The Importance of Being Ernest', directed by Maggie Davidson.

be the chancel curtain as the backdrop in the local parish church – a wonderful Gilbert Scott creation. The enormous audience would fill the clerestory and the back stalls would have pews available and superfluities would have to watch simultaneous transmission on a big screen at the local cricket pitch! Somewhere near 'cucumber sandwiches' preferably.

Seriously though – when the euphoria died down , it was agreed that I would play Algernon – in a north country accent and we found a traditional dainty character – very quicksilver – to play the other guy (Jack), the two leading characters. Cecily and Gwendolyn were played by two ladies with 'a certain majesty' of carriage. One was a student following the French course at the local polytechnic and the other worked for a petroleum company. We were a very mixed bag, very mixed indeed. We had a Jewish boy play Chasuble which was a nice touch and Miss Prism was played by possibly the youngest member of the whole cast. The idea was it was to be played seriously and it would be funny because of its seriousness. I shall come to other leading lights in this production as we go on. I can straightaway jump to a conclusion: the prompter was Maggie secretly in the pulpit and she of course had the biggest part on the day of the whole cast. We made one basic logistical mistake. One of the lads who you might think of as a Scottish rustic was to play the local bobby – is there a local bobby in that play? Well there is now! And he ran a wine shop and he generously provided refreshments before we began rehearsals. Well, just like The Greats, we had a fortifier and then a reinforcer and then a reassurer and the convivial 'one for the road' and rehearsals, as far as I know are still going on – this was tremendously as 10, 20, 30 years ago! The local paper mistook our intentions which was to get a bunch of journeymen together and put on an artisanal version of The Importance of Being Earnest which remains a tremendously funny play notwithstanding. We had the local shoe shop "geriatrics a speciality" shopkeeper, we had the other deli owner, we had another BP member – we didn't know what all of them did. They were probably" the missing members of MI6", so far as we knew.

However, we put this on under the blazon of THE ONE AND ONLY COMPANY and the whole idea was that it was to be done for one night only so we went round and drummed up our local shopkeepers to put an advert in our programme which was usually a sample of their business card which worked rather neatly and we eased through, 'Oh I'll help paint the scenery etc… to – have we got any scenery? (with a week to go). An interior mostly with ecclesiastical backdrops, that was our set, nicely raised up on rostrum level and the rest was either elevated in the upper storeys or slightly below that at audience level so the sight lines in this immense church were good. Nobody's ever counted but I suspect there'd be getting on for 200 people involved and that's without the people watching the big screen!

Off we went sweating blood of course. We took a helluva lot of prompts and I still don't know whose cigarette case was lost, purloined, mislaid or to be sought for and neither did my comrade in arms but we bantered around on the general themes of this cigarette case till the prompter – this mysterious voice from the pulpit – prophesied doom unless we gave a line by Oscar Wilde – which we, I think, did. It was honestly popular. The local bobby was there, the shopkeepers were there, people passing through were there. I was really banging the drum round the town recruiting an audience. We made scurrilous programmes illustrated with a Daulmier type carriage and posh people done by one of the cast. We had morning suits from the butler's sister who ran a hire shop, flowers in the buttonholes from somebody's garden and so on – it was all very openhearted. The local newspaper, as I said, misunderstood and thought we were some touring company from Kiev or somewhere and missed the point entirely to such an extent that we got the next local paper along to write an uncomplicated 'find as you see' criticism of the production which was casual, warmhearted and jolly. Why am I telling you this? Because the One and Only Company became the Two and Only Company in the next pub along and this time we put on John Mortimer's Marble Arch and A Resounding Tinkle by N F Simpson which I'd done on the QE2 (more later) so I sketchily gave it a prod from time to time by way of direction but the ingredients were there. We had an enormous rugby player as Uncle Ted in drag. More than this we managed to get – no names, no pack drill – a major 3 letter corporation connected with broadcasting worldwide make-up lady of considerable expertise to do the make-up which was sensational and we got Annie Hadley who was part of our circle

– yes, Annie Hadley who did the costumes for the Last Emperor and designs for grand opera in Brussels – she supported my idea that there wasn't enough money to buy fabric and took curtains (that was the next production – oh yes it doesn't end there) and with a bit of genius here there and everywhere made up magnificent costumes – I think this was for The Drunkard (a Victorian Melodrama) which could be snipped at crucial points and they would become curtains again so everybody was happy – a stunning tour de force – and we had a catwalk with her taking her bouquet of flowers at the end because she wanted to show off her new shoes – it was all pretty good. We put that on at the local primary school with gracious thanks to the Headmistress who was very helpful and same sort of reaction. People came of all sorts – but we were glad it was over to be honest. All the monies raised went to children's charities so there was no taint of jealousy or ego trips.

A good thing to do and an even better thing to have done! I contracted shingles in the course of the final production. God knows where it would have ended, had we done production number 27. We'd have run out of pubs on the same street, that's for sure. I still believe the audience would have turned up. In conclusion, I mention the mighty

Lady Bracknell who was played by Jean a retired English teacher with tremendous gusto and note that The Drunkard, the final production was a musical, provided on the pianoforte by Dave Thomas for "continuity" when we stopped…

In the garden of this House of Commons wallpapered pub, in a moment of frenzy, I put on a celebration to coincide with the investiture of Prince Charles as the Prince of Wales and it was called "Hooray for Charles the Third" no less.

There was a mound in the garden which made a natural sort of stage and quite an area of grass – not so much a lawn as a stretch of grassland which was a kind of natural open air theatre – in fact I understand that Regents Park Open Air is to review its arrangements as a consequence!

This play was mostly starring a pair of enormous toy ears bought by our leading man…they really were splendid and for some reason he had the features of the Heir to the Throne largely. Our players were all about 2' high (being young children) so it was amazing to rehearse them. It felt like talking to someone about half a mile away most of the time. However, it was brought to not so much perfection as to a realisable state and was put on in the garden on a beautiful sunny afternoon and the can for the children's charity was duly taken round and I understand a good time was had by all.

I say 'understand' because I was rehearsing at the time at the Acton Hilton a play with David Bowie called Baal, a sort of punk statement by Brecht directed by Alan Clarke, for television of course.

CHAPTER 17

WRITING

Writing has always been an abiding passion with me. I can remember my early works included the school essay on the Vale of Beaver (19/20), and a scrapbook about the tour on Vanguard to South Africa undertaken by the Princess Elizabeth and the Duke of Edinburgh, Prince Philip eg. That was very early on at school – a school project of some sort and I certainly wrote at primary school age (I remember because I did it when living at my grandmother's) reviews of the books that I'd read in an exercise book. All this is Sherlock Holmes stuff. It was just something you did. All this was when I was quite young.

But I never really got started and did not betray bits of my literature reading during my year in France. It was a foreign country obviously, a foreign language which put into sharp relief the value of precise English words I think partly and I think this is where the puns come from – this awareness of puns but also rhymes that had to accommodate themselves into the poem as a whole. I'd never done this before and I'd never done something so objective. Indeed, I'd never done anything so humorous before so this really was year 1. It took a year to write which is interesting in itself. I kept tinkering and going back to it but it doesn't rely on 'nudge, nudge, wink, wink' allusion to or feeding off other writers.

Herewith:

THE LAY OF THE LOST NOSTRIL

My self-coloured eyes hail Lily
Shipwrecked snug under the ether,
Stamped: "Venus Preserved" – for Billy
Oh asleep sterilised creature
Whiter vision of cellulose,
Nylon laundry mark, plastic nose.
In just any old peristyle
Down where the wild senapods bloom
I, Man made Fibrous,
Thou the while vivisectomy, my latex foam,
Anatomising all the night.
Fused in a blaze of bacolite.

Peter Davidson.

So this is the poem I came back with to England, to the Courtauld Institute and a fellow student there invited me to a poetry evening where we were obviously going to have interesting, fervent talks about poetry, we thought, so I went to this basement of a café somewhere in Knightsbridge and I believe it was run by Michael Horowitz with people reading their poems and it came round to my gap, and I read this poem which delighted people there and Horowitz asked if there were any more like that – he was obviously keen as well. The result was I went home and dashed off several poems similar in manner where the word play was paramount. I remember a Romeo and Juliet poem with broadside (lady's flank) coming into it. These poems were never read at these meetings. For some reason, I didn't go again but I think they probably reappeared in some form to do with my collage that I did fairly soon afterwards. So that was the first poem, certainly, I think.

When I was a student at the Courtauld, there was the foundation of the magazine YOU published on behalf of all universities in Britain and the editorship changed with each issue which was monthly. In the first issue of that there was a short story by John Le Carre and, as I remember, mine was the only poem published in it so that was a fairly wide audience, I imagine, for the same poem which is gratifying.

I then began writing stories as well as poems at home, for instance "The Recital" won LBC's short story competition and was broadcast nationwide (about a comically doomed piano recital in a small provincial town) Then I invented this character Spirelli, a sort of passe-partout. I wanted a fictional character who had all rights of passage. My mother-in-law's corsets were called Spirellas so I adapted that to Spirelli as a vaguely Italian presence, a fly by night you might say. He appears on a farm, in the army, as an academic sometimes, a champion snooker player and so on (Private Spirelli appears in the first issue of Guildford School of Art's Magazine – Nexus) a catalyst to enter into a hitherto forbidden world and just get on with it like a native – he's very very useful, is Spirelli... I also invented the South Mimms School for foreigners who want to learn English: SMSFFWWTLE for short and we had all sorts of characters from all sorts of places, not least on the staff list producing "knowing slapstick" as one reviewer put it about this amazing institution. It has now been wholly taken over by expansion on behalf of the service station.★

★Talking about service stations, I did hear that South Mimms and other service stations are not on the M25. In other words, when the M25 was first established, there were no service stations on it. It was at the time of Thatcher's

Government and the story was that she built it to take mobile guided missiles. I've worked it out – it's about 135 miles of road so they wouldn't need a service station, would they so, unimpeded, these vehicles would possibly have circulated 24/7 in some form and provide a genuine threat to an aggressor coming in with guided missiles.

Just a thought…!

Spirelli had quite a few adventures and we did stage quite a few dramas at the South Mimms School for Foreigners who want to Learn English. These are all on audio cassette with all the characters voiced by me, which was a fun thing to do.

There were poems between these strands, as they say, about all sorts of things – Christmas time giving way to social aggression after the holiday had finished, a lot of Thatcher targeting when she first came to power and me being in education, she seemed an enormous threat to the way of life that had burnished British thinking in many ways. All this pursuit of the lowest common denominator – everybody's included i.e. will pay tax and so on. It seemed so cynical at the time so one poem I remember talked about 'the last hospice bed, surveyed by a man smoking a big cigar!' – that kind of blatant outrage – outrage is a good word but they covered all sorts of things including The Loch Ness Monster. So I suddenly realised that I was getting more satisfied in the poems I was writing in particular but I wrote a lot of short stories about the various places I found myself in fundamentally. In other words, there was a grain of truth, a big grain of truth in everything I'd written.

I did some copywriting for false eyelashes for that exhibition I mentioned I did in Brighton then a poem about the perversity of writing copy which I hoped atoned for my misdemeanour in writing it.

> There's a black dog follows me around,
> made of plastic that cannot burn.

It's very self flagellatory I suppose but I had no feedback about it. Nobody said 'you rotter, you shouldn't have charged us a penny'; as far as I know it was a success in what it tried to do. There were various bits of copywriting for women's journals and papers and one for the stand on which it was displayed and so on. It was a good thing to do or to have done – the same old thing. A bit like O Level, really. Talking of which, O Level at my school was a pretty comprehensive thing – I did 8 in the end including late ones, like picking up a third language at University. But I enjoyed the syllabuses – I'm glad I did the whole range of work, for it wasn't just pounds, shillings and pence, not just a method. There was an element of enquiry in the science for instance in the lab work. It was speculative as well as repetitive so I wouldn't knock O Level as a basis for assessment of pupils at the right age of course.

So these O levels were accompanied by the moaning poems – long lines and little else – but sympathetically listened to by one of my housemasters so that was one way of getting through the school day. Dylan Thomas was another and the last poem I wrote before 'The Lay of the Lost Nostril' was laced with Dylan Thomasisms, to the poem's benefit I might say but they stand out rather vividly once you're tuned to that idea.

GOODNIGHT LITTLE TOWN

Goodnight little town,
Huddle of whispers and herons dropping down the sky
Lost in a wave of hills
that heave like whales in a frost glitter sea.
The clanking workmen hammer smoke,
ambling up to the battleship clouds,
riding quiet in the helter-skelter of your runaway dusk.

Feet pass stamping back up the street
and secret mist is stalking the stone cattle
Humped on the grey fields.

Peter Davidson

This kind of Romanticism is not lost but, rather, added to in things written after The Lay of the Lost Nostril.

So, The Lay of the Lost Nostril, the first poem where I've shaken off my thoughts about various 'lits' and written a poem of my own – an important landmark, kind of pushed into the background by circumstances and then gets going hot and strong in my 20's when I think nothing of getting up in the middle of the night and writing a poem that was tapping at the bedroom door. It became a much greater pleasure as well. I tend normally to write very quickly. I may cross out a lot but I write very quickly. This year long catharsis of the old style was absolutely necessary but not a typical way of working. I've never picked up a poem, I don't think, shall we say a year later and finished it or anything like that. Some writing is a transposition of dreams the next morning – very vivid but often very strong in narrative and complete in their subject so I recollected them as best I could and made a poem or short story out of them. These tend to be often strong in eroticism.

Translation I've done very seldom and just once in a while I've written in French in particular a poem. It's not become established as something I do but I think I might. I'm still haunted by a fine translation I'm looking for 'L'Ecume des Jours', Boris Vian's novel which I know in English as 'Froth on the Daydream' which seems to me a start but 'spume' would be an improvement already but I'm thinking of different ideas – 'Descant on the Humdrum' is one suggestion. I'm still working on it.

The band 'Flutacious` who do live gigs and distribute discs widely heard my poem 'Open Window' which is what it says, for out outside the window there are all sorts of rich noises: building construction, a river, cats, birds and all the panoply. They heard this, liked it and it made them compose a piece called 'Open Window' which lasts about a quarter of an hour and actually incorporates a reading of the poem, sometimes spread out as it were – fragments of the poem repeated. I think this is very good and enjoyable and flattering. Such a collaboration I hope might expand.

I have already married visuals with my writing notably in the DVD 'Together' where shots of landscapes or abstract things are mixed with some poems. This has done particularly well, especially in places like The Arts Council Poetry Library where, it's reported, it's forever being taken out which is gratifying and they applauded that it was essentially one poet's work without technical assistance from outside.

So, all these strands are waiting to be pursued in some way perhaps.

I am still attracted very much by the essay as a format. When I was working on the Environmental Design Course in an art school, the Head of Dept. asked me to write something about water and this rather unleashed me and I started off with the purity of it in terms of sacraments and so on and its usefulness as a source of power and also a source of pleasure. It was called 'Water, Purity – Power and Pleasure' and was illustrated with a fairground car coming to the watersplash at the end of the ride on the big dipper at Battersea. First of all with somebody just holding tight so to speak, protecting themselves against the water and followed by someone sticking their hand out in the spray generated by the car which seems to have a lot of joy in it.

I also was asked to present a piece on speaking English for the World Service. I had done plays: Andorra for the World Service for instance and Precious Bane for Radio 3 and The Book of Marjorie Kemp for Radio 3 which brought me up against directors like Walter da Costa, Piers Plowright and Vanessa Whitburn. I had also done at least 200 pieces of voice work including the poems for Television South West's tribute to Thomas Hardy which again was flattering to be chosen. So I regard it as a medium I'm at home in and enjoyed doing that. It was totally original really – an example: – in a crossword, the clue is forbears and everyone took it to mean "indulges" but, in fact, with the stress on the first syllable it means "ancestors". So it was about stress in English and the importance of it and it's also about nilogisms introduced from foreign speakers. I liked one from a German friend who was worried that a man involved in an argument in a pub was going to "aggress" his mate, which I will certainly keep at the back of my mind. Anyway, this was broadcast all over the world and heard definitely by a filmmaker friend of mine in Africa who gave me feedback on it!

I enjoy voice work for you have to conjure up the scene you're presenting.

Of course, I hear all my own work in my head, before it's written down.

By the same token, I've naturally given "performances" of my writing in a room above a pub where there's a chance to 'act out' the full meaning and receive instant feedback. In some of these, I was joined on the bill by Alan Franks – satirical "folk songs" to his own accompaniment on guitar or banjo and the singer Patti Veta. All were enthusiastically received.

THIEF

Smithereens of once upon a time fishes
slop on the riverbank
or lie rusting in the sun.
The brown bear's jagged lunge
splinters the river's stainless steel surfaces.
His bloody rainbow, nevertheless, gives this
Innocent
Half a halo.

Peter Davidson

CHAPTER 18

ABU DHABI AND DUBAI

A little de luxe theatre.

There now follows a sort of intermezzo, a time to dream sequence, a soma holiday, if you like, and time out of mind in many ways. I'm going to describe for you the journey we made with drama on the QE2 eventually. It's what you might call an interval entertainment.

I heard about this far away places little tour to the Middle East from my agent and decided to go for it. I went to see the director, Richard Felgate, and he told me what they were going to do which was to put on one act plays in the theatres of very 5 star hotels in Abu Dhabi and Dubai so I was auditioning for 5 leading roles with an all expenses paid trip to put on one performance of each of these and see the world at the same time so I went for it, really did go for it and Richard said, "Oh I like what I see," and promptly cast me in the roles. So I went to French's and got the texts and retired to the Coal Hole Pub on the Strand to see what I'd landed and it was 'pretty good... pretty good'.

We flew to the Arab Emirates and put on these plays that I'm sure I mentioned (John Mortimer, N. F. Simpson, Neil Simon etc.) and flew back again picking up on the way this wonderful review: "P.J. Davidson's energy is astounding and

nan plan
or 4,278
ow-cost
houses

'AT—Oman news-
aid in yesterday's issue
ie Ministry of Social
and Labour was plan-
set up new 4,278 low-
uses at a cost of 40 mil-
nani Rials. The project
be carried out over the
/e years.

₹ 1981, the Ministry would
/10 residential units in the
areas, Rostaq, Buraimi,
Bani Bu Ali, Thamreet,
im, Hima and Liwa.
2—652 housing units will be
alalah, Awabi, Bidayya, Ibra,
oura and Bahla.
83, the Ministry will build
esidential units in Qabil,
cki, Soweiq and Sur, in addi-
ie capital area. In 1984, 440
al units will be constructed in
umail, Masanaa, Nizwa and

finistry's plan is part of the
ent's efforts to provide ade-
using facilities to the citizens.
irst five-year plan enabled
an 3,000 families to obtain
houses built by the ministry.
.l cost of the project was 15
)mani Rials.
ewspaper also said that the
of Electricity and Water was
g its five-year plan. Costing
50 million Omani Rials, the
rget is to provide electricity
²r to citizens in various dis-
would he launched early next

Peter Davidson and Pat Kneale as mother and father in the "Visitor from Forest Hills" at Hyatt's dine-in theatre.—Khaleej Times photo

40pc Emirtel shares for nationals

THE Ministry of Communica-
tions will submit to the Council of Ministers next month a
memorandum proposing that
the nationals be offered 20 per
cent shares of Emirtel which
the government has bought
from two foreign companies.

This will raise to 40 per cent
national's share in the organisation's

Entertainment in search of audience

By Staff Reporter

THERE had to be a time when
Dubai's entertainment band-
wagon became overloaded.
For a long time now it has been

particularly true of "Forest Hills" in
which Peter Davidson played an out-
raged father whose daughter becomes
terrified of her pending wedding and
lockes herself in the bathroom. His
energetic performance nearly suc-
ceeded in overcoming the obstacles of

Report in the Khaleej Times – Abu Dhabi & Dubai, Roy Hubley
in Plaza Suite with Pat Kneale, by Neil Simon.

redeems the entire production almost (or something a little
less effervescent) "Sharjah Times". These places were not fully
developed as resorts. They were a kind of Stonehenge these
Hyatt Regency Hotels in lone sandhills drifting away to the
sea which was always the same colour because the sun always
shone exactly the same. I think it was April. Everything was
exactly the same colour so we had these monoliths rising up
with windows quadruple glazed against the nearby airport. I
remember looking out of my bedroom window and seeing a
plane you could virtually shake hands with making scarcely any

noise at all. I remember beef bacon, thinly sliced beef pretending to be bacon rather than pork, which is where we find ourselves in a Muslim country. Drink was absolutely out but I remember seeing in the foyer of our hotel the "Sheik of Arabee" – 12' tall in his white robes – drinking what looked like a triple whiskey with a solitary mournful chunk of ice – I guess there are ways. You keep hearing reports of the municipality bulldozing bottles of whiskey into the sand dunes or that kind of thing.

So that's about it. We were consigned to this air conditioned hotel. There was a pool with a wind sail surfer sitting on it, looking around for customers, which I nearly went on and I did flap around in the sea for five minutes and got some ear infection and the doctor gave me penicillin, saying if I drank a couple of whiskeys I might as well forget the penicillin. It was £34 for a couple of consultations plus the medicine which was paid for eventually back in London. That's all I honestly do remember about it, except the stuff of legend, like a big fat paperback called 'Dubai'. Later of course there was this tremendous explosion – entertainment in Abu Dhabi and Dubai! We went between the two in a coach, had a cup of coffee in the desert in the middle – interesting of course. Otherwise we shared a room, two of us in each case – 6 members in our troupe. It really went quite well for a short time. We visited a girl who was running an English radio station, during this trip, but, other than that, it was time out of mind. It was just good food, 'tout confort' (every convenience), 5 star treatment in a foreign land which was fascinating for a short time and the plays, being such a rarity in those places, went down very well indeed but it was a bit unnerving hearing the knives and forks being pushed away or placed on plates at the end of what was the dinner aspect of this dinner/theatre experience they were having – hiding behind the arras, waiting for the play to begin, listening to the munch, munch of the diners before the play started. It was a kind of splendid dessert, a live dessert I suppose, at the end of their gala dinner that we were doing.

This was followed by an invitation to play the same and more parts on the QE2.

So I had an evening suit from a second hand costumier (cost me 30 shillings) which was obligatory for shaking hands with the Captain. This is what I meant when I said the various strands began to intertwine. When I began to work as a film extra, they insisted that everyone had an evening suit to stand in the distance of something like Casino Royale. So there I was wearing my extras evening suit that had lapels you could land a jumbo jet on. They were either a brand new custom made outfit by Savile Row Tailors for a pop star or the outfit worn by James Cagney when he was taller. There I was discovered on the cross they had chalked on the deck for me to stand on so my features would be favoured and the Captain would be a little more in profile as he shook my hand and welcomed me on board – long as he didn't say, "You're in the Queen's Navy, Mr. Christian," I was happy. My suit appealed to my inverted snobbery. I loved getting away with something amidst all this jewellery that was real and a £1000 worth of suit walking around – all that kind of thing – terrific!

CHAPTER 19

QE2.

I had seen very big ships before when I was a boy in Liverpool of course – the Mauritania as a troop ship, the Queen Elizabeth – things like that. But I'd never been near a really big ship like that, so near its water line looking up and along such an immensity . I worked it out and it really is – to within inches – the length of Winchester Cathedral navigating itself to within 3 ft of where it actually is travelling along across the World at 45 miles an hour.

Imagine, if you will, a bunch of ragged thespians looking at this ship, this QE2 as they prepare to embark and voyage half way round the World with interesting stops on the way. This is what, essentially, it was. We flew to Singapore to pick up the QE2. Singapore was really a bus stop so we did 'bus stoppy' things. We went to a teashop and, to our dismay, were served a teabag, which was not what we'd expected at all i.e. dancing girls and sweet music and things – not a bit of it, so we came out into a shower or hot bath which is Singapore – humidity 0.1 off 100% and went to the nearest Raffles and its fans and beautiful green and cream harmonious decor and its Singapore Slings. We enjoyed them all pretty equally and felt much better about the Far East.

The next day, we climbed up the ladder to this block of

flats or housing estate called the QE2 and quickly found our accommodations. These are shared two people at a time. They are airy, spacious, twin beds, a porthole to look out of, in this case and a wardrobe, wash basin, bath, shower, toilet –just enough for what we were going to do which was to have a 5 week holiday. Each day there was a competition on the QE2 to guess the number of miles travelled on a particular day – I don't remember the exact distance travelled in a day because it didn't feel like travelling at all. On one occasion, when it was very rough – it could have been the Bay of Biscay – I think the stabilisers were rolled out. You could hear them thundering out to stabilise the ship but it didn't make you feel queasy at all. It pitched and rolled to some degree. I remember going down to one of the swimming pools and the water was at the lip of the walking surface at the top and was virtually at the bottom at the other end – a tilt par excellence – but not felt underfoot. On top of everything else, the cabins were very quiet – beautifully insulated. I don't think every cabin has a window – oh porthole, must be careful – to look out of and see the passing seagulls.

The Seychelles was the first time we felt we were doing something special. We found ourselves on a silvery beach, looking at today's catch – all the colours of the rainbow and at a turquoise sea that you could see the bottom of (quite deep really) and a matching sky, a gentle breeze, palm trees with coconuts on. It was like a Bounty advert. We sat in the sea, that's about all you could manage, it was so hot – the sea itself was on the verge of being too hot. One of the artistes in the crowd (there was about 20 of us) on the beach sported a pair of blue 'y' fronts probably by Damian Hurst – who knows? Perhaps he thought there would be no sea on a five week cruise halfway round the World. Anyway, it was torpid, just enough breeze to keep consciousness and we sat there and did nothing at all except work out how to stand up again at the end of an hour or so. Fantastic – we really had arrived.

Mombasa – a town on the coast of Kenya – beautiful, smart town, not far away from the Kenya Safari Park which we had planned to see the next day. We got up early, went out in a little coach and there we were, getting up at the same time as the lions – a leopard we saw, zebra, elephants on the horizon, a giraffe – all these animals doing what came naturally to them. Way below – it seemed 1000 feet, a river. It was a gorge going down to a plateau with crocodiles basking on the sandbanks, the size of telegraph poles at least – quite unbelievable. It was awesome, awesome. There was an enormous thunderstorm – from horizon to horizon – while we were there. It bucketed down, it really did. When it went away, we looked for places to dry our shirts – a hedge or somebody's topiary – no way. But we suddenly realised our shirts were dry from the sun that had come out again! Amazing! And we lounged around for the rest of the day.

I remember going to the swimming pool on the top deck, knotting my handkerchief at each corner and putting it on my head as you do at Skeggie. Of course everybody laughed and pointed and tee-heed but I was the one that wasn't sweating blood with sunstroke at dinnertime. Great days. Everything you could desire really plus the usual conveniences : a bank, a library which was quite a small room, a casino which was quite a big room, dance floor, several restaurants, several swimming pools, a shop that sold all sorts, not just souvenirs. My sainted aunt, it was something! You could just wander about it for days on end. The Chinese laundry personnel never left the ship – ever!

As strolling vagabonds, we had no particular class. We were not allowed in the first class restaurant but we were allowed in the stokers' bar where the ship's currency – dollars – would buy an Aswandamful of lager or thereabouts. We were invited to the officers' wardroom and there we found the 'wrens' – the officers, radio operators and so on – women. All of them looked as if they would win the decathlon, never mind the heptathlon – very smart, very good looking. There they were, skirts held up, bouncing around on child of 3 or 4 size wooden horses, round the painted racetrack on the deck and they were being betted upon by the male (I nearly said chauvinists) but they were certainly on their own and in their own thing, leaning against the bar making wagers on these serf like girls. I understand that this facility was opened by Germaine Greer but I don't believe it!!

On, to sundecks. I remember getting up very early one day by mistake, having a hamburger with all the trimmings for breakfast and watched a man who might have been a maharaja in his khaki shorts doing Tai Chi or one of those things to the amazement of two or three onlookers and a jogger who looked like he might be on his last legs to me. You can imagine a lap of the ship's deck was quite a lot, to say nothing of avoiding deckchairs where the hardy were wrapped up in sleeping bags and blankets, "taking the sun" don't ye know "taking the sun" Ah me!

The dances were good and free for all, come-as-you are. Peter Gordeno who is a dance choreographer of course said to me, "you can't dance but you can move," and I won the record for the best backhanded compliment of the day.

It was the days of Tequila Sunrise at sunset, the days of lager at the musicians bar, tall tales and glazed eyes as we smiled benignly on anyone who would pay attention. Not really but it was relaxed to the nth – an ideal holiday. Time out of mind.

After Mombasa we went to Djibuti to refuel I believe – a relatively poor standard of living there compared to Mombasa.

One of our troupe, putting on a blue rinse accent and a fixed grin said 'They might be poor but they don't have to be dirty.' I don't know if that's PC but it's as PC as the ladies' horse race in the wardroom that's for sure.

We went through the Suez Canal with about a foot of water either side of the ship – seriously – which was intriguing. We went to Port Said and everything the soldiers said was true and there's still a man thrusting invitations to a sort of gymkhana where a donkey does tricks with a rather comely lady of the town we're told.

Egypt and the surrounding area left me pretty cold. It's like all the colours on a palette mixed together. It's just been modelled out of clay and that's all there is to it. I didn't, I must say, visit its nightlife and all those things.

The Pyramids – once you've seen one... no, I had my photograph taken with my Cunard QE2 t-shirt by a little boy I gave some money to. They are bigger than me, those blocks, in height, to say nothing of length. We had to wait for this treat because 3 black limousines that looked as if they, as well as all the party with about 20 besuited people, were wearing dark, dark sunglasses. Apparently Colonel Gadaffi had come to pay a visit – salute perhaps something he regards as his patrimony. Impressive enough but, you know, you don't go away with very much in my personal opinion. I emphasise however I did not see the Valley of the Kings or Carnac or any of the supreme heights of Egyptology.

Whilst in that part of the world, we went to Jerusalem. To get there from the coast we were taken in a coach, a full sized coach with an Israeli guide who spoke mostly about the Arab-Israeli War but he mentioned this and that and passed round about a hundred slides for I forget how much and foolishly passed the whole 100 round for us to see in a box so people shuffled through and on occasion took out what they fancied and he was prepared to bring down all the ancient Gods and contemporary ones on he who had committed a felony if the box was not returned FULL!, by the time one circuit was completed.

I did find a moment of peace on this trip – a strange tranquillity, as if everything had been switched off and I asked him what this place was and he said – strangely quietly – 'This is the Garden of Gethsemane.' This was a vivid and powerful experience – far more to me than the rather Madame Tussaud Birth of Christ place (stable). But Jerusalem did redeem itself. I did walk on the Via Dolorosa but with everybody else but two things surpassed everything – The Dome on the Rock – the Blue Mosque it must be, azure lapis lazuli dome, traced through with gold. It is quite unspeakably magnificent. The other thing is a landscape round the River Jordan which suddenly puts you in a Bellini painting – those paintings of the north Italian countryside with the Madonna and Child in the foreground – that kind of colour that's on the way to becoming full blown – extraordinary nuance rather than contrast. The River Jordan – absolutely beautiful, that particular aspect of it anyway. Cairo looks like it's been modelled out of clay and left to dry but I didn't visit the hotspots. Cairo Museum – great to see the death mask of Tutankhamun twice – once as shotgun for an American Express guided tour. They discovered I was a guide and asked me to watch the end of the group as we went round and once with the crew tour. But once you've seen emeralds and things displayed on brown paper which is amazing – startling to start with. It almost becomes a Ratner sale as time goes on so I'm not getting much out of my tour apart from a soma holiday – time out of mind but we went to Athens and I stood in the middle of the Parthenon, looked down on Athens and towards where Athena was and round at the sculpture much of which is original, still in place and felt the scale of it which is exactly the relationship of yourself to the Gods which the Greeks esteemed and were so very proud of. It's something else – not quite something else entirely because if you go to The British Museum, you will see some of the original pieces of sculpture and Triglyths and Metops but also you will be in the Duveen Room which is the size of the Parthenon deliberately made so. In diagrammatic form you will have something of that experience.

The air and the light hit you in Athens like the curtain opening in a magnificent theatre to a fully lit set, the air is just the right temperature, the light is just beautiful and everything is visible in its entirety somehow, even miles and miles away – these lovely white buildings. Everything delineated against that incredibly heavy but split sapphire sky. Ah! The cradle I suppose of our European civilisation.

We went to Palermo, the capital of course of Sicily. That was the only landfall we made 'in Italy' but it was relaxing and impressive at the same time, the marvellous cathedral in the square where there is also a taverna where we all had a glorious meal. There was the casino croupier, some stewardess ladies, some of the physical, naval crew as it were and of course our troupe of merry men who I must think of a title for… quite fun to call them the muffins since we spent most of the time eating and were ragged compared to your average professional tourist. Right, the Muffins. So we had this excellent meal with wine and at the end, a rather comely lady came in and looked round the table, finally sat on my knee and kissed me. These Sicilians you know, they're passionate.

We were to make a landfall in Tunisia or thereabouts and see a camel race but the weather was not permitting a thing of that size to get anywhere near the shore at the time so we zoomed on to Gibraltar which reminded me strangely of Dover

Castle and Dover's fortifications and of course the monkeys with whom I felt a fellow feeling because we were rehearsing my 'chef d'oeuvre' with the cast of muffins, some of the crew and artistes – a pianist and singers from all the bands who were not allowed to play together as a musical ensemble. There were 5 musicians who'd been doing various recitals of dance music throughout the cruise.

My 'chef d'oeuvre' as I call it, was an episode of This is Your Life starring the trombonist from the ship's conservatoire of musicians, introduced by the Alan Wicker look-a-like – of course wearing James Cagney's cast off evening suit. There were no prompts, as we all read from the script, as is traditional with One and Only Touring Companies. It was a bit kitchen sink with a muffin as his Mum washing the outside step with her choicest underwear (where else would you find a cloth on the QE2?) Other delights included the pianist facing Billingham instead of the audience and £50 collected for the ship's charity, for children. The audience were mostly the crew who responded well, especially to the idea of the 5 'ringfenced' singers who closed the show with "When The Saints Go Marching In" as an ensemble.

One of the bandleaders videoed it all – it's probably in a time capsule on the Moon by now (tickets still available).

I almost forgot Sri Lanka. We visited Kandi and Colombo, saw elephants hauling tree trunks about and a snake charmer among a sort of mosaic of wonderful saris against the lush green of the landscape. I'm still digesting the hottest curry known to Man!

CHAPTER 20

HIGH POINTS

Moments that have singled themselves out in four and a half careers and many odd jobs. A sporting moment which I won't forget came when we had a triangular match as I recall between Glasgow, Edinburgh and Aberdeen plus Queens and Trinity. We travelled overnight sorting out the world on a ferry from Glasgow to northern Ireland with a mixture of the athletes from the teams so the discussion was very lively and animated with various exercises thrown in – shot putters doing their thing with their arms, pole vaulters doing theirs which was quite unnerving. Anyway we landed eager, bright eyed and sleepless in Belfast and were amazed to find how well we felt. Belfast is a very relaxed place I found with an almost serenity (early 60's) without being boring. I was immediately impressed by the University buildings – Queens University which is mixed traditionally compared to a lot of Oxford and Cambridge colleges which probably contributed a lot to the feeling of relaxation.

Anyway we had a meal there and did our duty on the sports field. I believe it was the next day because we'd had quite a bit of Guinness by this time – it was a kind of Grinning Holiday to us so we did our duty although there was a bit of diminution of performance but this was a mere rehearsal for the competition the next day in Dublin. The placings were the same as they normally would be according to past performance so honour remained satisfied and pleasure abundantly so. Juvenes Dum Sumus, as they say.

At the dance at the end of the day I and a lot of our team mixed in with dances we were not all that familiar with so largely we invented. I engaged in conversation with an extremely pretty girl who finally said, 'No.'

Happy times, happy times…

We got up a bit bleary eyed to go to Dublin. Things that surprised me for example – Customs men coming on the train and seizing the News of the World exclusively it seemed from our little compartments of 4 or 6 and stuffing them in a briefcase they appeared to have brought for the purpose.

We arrived in Dublin and straight away the sea made an enormous impact right next to the city and a feeling of antiquity, a feeling of venerability struck me I must say. Trinity College seemed a bit more serious, a bit more academic. But this was soon dispelled. The athletics were particularly jubilant as the performances went down… and the placements remained the same.

The real excitement came after the whole match. Before we started you remember, it was discus my main event, we had a throw around and a chap in a green tracksuit threw casually a discus off the athletics field as such and into some long grass. It took us a while to find it and even longer to find an explanation for this phenomenal (much bigger than ours) throw. It came soon enough. He turned around and across the back of his green tracksuit, written in gold letters, was UGANDA – q.e.d.

The competition continued and Mr. Uganda invited us for a drink and a bit of food at his place which was nice so we went round and at half past 4 in the morning, having set the world to rights yet again and eating an amazing curry made of oodles of grains and millions of spices and what seemed honestly to be a tin of sardines (quite biblical really) – there must have been 8 of us in the room – we finally called it a night and listened hard for the chimes at midnight and 'none came nigh us.

I was sharing a room with a high jumper from Cheshire equally – a very nice openhearted chap and we agreed we were going to kip like logs which we did for the very short time and then got ready to leave for an early plane back. So we returned with a Guinness drinking record including the climax at Brendan Behan's favourite pub with a grin on our faces and a song in our heart. Gaudeamus igitur.

The most exciting acting experience I've had is the occasional time when you suddenly realised that an audience is not really there. They've been transported to the play. It's an unnervingly wonderful feeling of power and again immense relaxation and justification – pleasure on their behalf. You really feel you've made it worthwhile – that must be one of the world's great sensations. I can't single out any experience in acting as exhilarating as those moments, except I've always liked Spike Milligan and I played The Thing in the film of Spike Milligan's 'Adolph Hitler, My Part in his Downfall'. This was an Army improvised boxing match between Jim Dale and me. We improvised round a very skeleton script a boxing match. I was twice everything he put on the canvas ring – twice the weight, twice the width and twice as gormless. He was marvellous to improvise with. He was the nippy 'Oh my God' and I was 'Is this what I do?' thump thump gorilla like strikes. We went round and round and round to the delight of Joan Bakewell who said in an article that we were the greatest thing she'd seen since 'Champion Charlie' starring Charlie Chaplin. It was great. It was like writing a play and performing

'The Thing' with Jim Dale at The Boxing Match. Film – 'Adolph Hitler, My Part In His Downfall' by Spike Milligan, directed by Norman Cohen.

on the first night yourself – a tremendous experience although I'd not slept the night before for thinking about it. We got our photographs in Photoplay and things like that – it was separated out (this boxing match) as a moment of real verve. Arthur Lowe was in it and other actors of that kind which made a terrific audience for Jim and me. Bob Todd was the referee – it was his first lesson as a referee having cut his toenails to fit into his boxing boots. All sorts of little knickknacks. I remember somebody who escaped the scrutiny of the director sitting bang slap in the middle of camera foreground for the lower angle shots which would be very telling with a haircut that looked like a sphynx, triangular over his ears. I'm sure if he'd leant forward abruptly he'd have taken off into the middle of the ring so those had to be abandoned in the rushes. Nonetheless the whole ring collapsed as the audience swarmed onto it to the astonishment of all concerned not least the director – a movement of some brio… So that was a good acting experience.

Guiding Memory/ies:

Surfing up the contiguous roundabouts, mini roundabouts up a hill near Salisbury on the way back from Stonehenge – this was with Bob a particularly talented coach driver who became a haulier and his own boss. We did it more than once, it took perfection to be fully satisfactory. He'd slam it into probably third gear and this very powerful coach would use half a tank of fuel getting up these incredible figure-skating circles as it were and I gave a racing commentary into the mike as we went along. We were all covered in sweat when we got to the top and our tea, not least a man from Ohio, mopping his brow with a handkerchief that said 'ohio, ohio, ohio' on it. We earned our tea.

The other bit of guiding in which we guided ourselves was at the end of Humphrey's momentous journey, five weeks,

Round Trip 45' Turning Circle, Top speed 46mph up the hill, down the dale, called the Alps to Rome (Morris 8) and we took ourselves first of all to be wowed by the Sistine Chapel. I've never breathed for three minutes on so little breath in my whole life – it was momentous in detail and all in all a quite stunning experience! When you consider I had looked at it piece by piece, centimetre by centimetre in the History of Art Course so recently, the impact was stunning, literally stunning.

I think the highlights of teaching were the feeling of immense contact evinced from time to time when the students gave me something they valued because they thought I'd be interested in it, things like a Polish Olympic poster from a Polish student or a photograph, an etching and so on. Also I wrote a list of what I'd personally enjoyed for students using my newly established library at Worthing and it was considerable in all sorts of categories. I remember saying: 'If you'd like to recommend something to me, do,' and it was excellent because this particular student recommended 'A Clockwork Orange' which I later saw on the stage and in the cinema and every time I saw it, I would remember that moment and probably give people a rerun of the event.

Chapter 21

Serious Acting.

I was very lucky at the beginning of my London acting experience to be cast for Trevor Griffiths' "Bill Brand" with Jack Shepherd in the eponymous part. Trevor is so accessible and direct in what he does, it's a joy to rehearse, let alone to perform his work. But it was a glorious cast as well – Geoffrey Palmer, Arthur Lowe, Ray Smith and Alan Badel! Mustn't rhapsodise too much. Alan Badel is the only actor that I've come out of the theatre and been

'Bill Brand' by Trevor Griffiths – The Conference Scene,
directed by Stuart Burge.

Alan Badel – Michael Foot with his PPS.

Mr. Leivers with family in 'Sons and Lovers',
adapted by Trevor Griffiths, directed by Stuart Burge.

of one mind with Maggie that we should immediately book better, nearer to the stage seats. This is what happened to his "Kean". It was so unbelievably good that we went back and saw him in close-up a couple of days afterwards I think, having had to wait for the appropriate seat. So to be cast as Alan Badel's Parliamentary Private Secretary (he was leader of the Labour Party) in the play about the Labour Party Conference was more than a treat – it was incredible. I'm still reeling under the company I kept. Subsequently we went out to the end of the District Line – I can't even remember the name of the place – (Hornchurch?) – to see Seymour Mathews play in "Comedians" (also by Trevor) which was really something. Bill Brand has a cunningly concealed sub-plot. It's an unfinished game of chess in the wings fought out by Jack Shepherd and me. We have the same sort of level as chess players i.e 'what?' We've worked out that one of us is white and one of us is black but no further – to be continued I hope. Everything about that production was terrific. Apart from everything else, Alan Badel turned out to be a really amiable man which I thought was surprising considering the majesty, one could almost say. The sort of guy that invites you into his brand new Renault 16 royal blue limousine to join him for fish and chips – you can't say fairer than that.

The upshot of all these good vibrations is that, when I saw a few years later that Stuart Burge, who had directed Bill Brand was going to direct an adaptation of Sons and Lovers, also by Trevor Griffiths, I was emboldened to ask Trevor by postcard if he thought there might be something in his production for me... eventually I played Miriam's father which was a delightful part. The family aspect of this was Tom Bell played Mr. Morell, Eileen Atkins Mrs. Morell, Jean Boht played my wife Mrs Leivers and I played Mr. Leivers and our daughter was Leonie Mellinger. We filmed in the studio of course and the delightful rustic setting in the Peak District of Derbyshire. My father was helpful in this. He

'Stepan' in 'Black Beauty', with Bill and Blaise (Black Beauty)
in a 'run-thru'! Directed by Charles Crichton.

was born in Nottinghamshire and was a fan of D.H.Lawrence
understandably in any case. And he very kindly made a tape of a
conversation he had with a farmer about my age and vintage as a
character which I found very helpful to get rid of the rough edges
I had. Remember I spent my evacuation in Derbyshire so I had a

flying start with that one. There was a tremendous affection for it. I remember when our family was getting together for a scene, Trevor said at one rehearsal, "The Leivers are massing!" It was very close-knit and congenial and very effective I felt. To cap it all, my eldest 'son' – the precocious one – filled a lull with; 'If God had intended us to go around with no clothes on, he'd have given me a bigger willie!' – jubilation all round. I've since recorded D.H. Lawrence's poems which gives you some idea of the dedication I have for D.H. Lawrence so that was an abundantly good experience.

The horse we had in Sons and Lovers was gentle and obliging, not so "my" horses in 'Black Beauty'. Judy Bowker was playing the heroine and Bill Lucas was her father and we were in Rickmansworth and the idea was I should be the bodyguard, deaf mute, just to be handy, of the duchess in a fantastic tale of kidnap and bad men coming in from Europe such as Bernard Achard streaking across the fields in his cape blowing in the wind and that kind of gothic feel to it as well.

Well, I was to be the coachman, the sentry, all sorts of things in the protection of the duchess. So we thought – Reg Dent who was the horseman and I (but mostly Reg Dent) that we should rehearse these horses – Bill and Blaise who I think had been finally laid off from the Circus Maximus – I say this because they weren't kids in arms and one of them was quite a lot of hands and the other one was even more so. Once harnessed together they would have gone round in some sort of ellipse by just walking straight which would explain a few things but rather more like the orbit of Jupiter I would suggest than the circuit of the Circus Maximus – stroke of genius. There was a rather steep field with very long grass in it so Reg said, "Let's start gently," so the horses were standing still nicely and I said, as instructed, "Walk on," and they ambled along perfectly, not noticing the incline and the rough grass they were going on. They were strong as hell. When we got to the top, they decided to speak only Esperanto or whatever and set off flat out vaguely hysterical and this is where the swimming pool became the final destination of my ambition. The horseman cantered nicely up to them, got hold of the nosey bit of reins and inveigled them to a nice stop, more or less on somebody's foot. Oh yes. This seeming resolution was counterpointed in the Duchess's fried egg roll going into a tiny orbit in the coach, then making a soft landing on her silk dress which cost more weeks wages than we could count to. She said something I didn't quite catch but a bale of hay almost burst into flames nearby.

I think I more than atoned for it with my balletic performance with the Ghost in Hamlet (see later).

It is true that, as time went on, I did become a bit diffident about lines. For instance, even in 'the king', which if you look at it, is very rapid fire. Mercifully the Clerk – Nigel Betts – was very happy to belt through our lines together, which is the whole of the 2nd Act, at the interval so I came on reading my lines through my imagination pointing at the recently performed script in my

Read through of 'The Pixie Led' by Christopher Harris.

head. It was a great service and I've done this for other people. It's strange isn't it that people who are very intelligent I may say and fluent in other ways need that little something perhaps as time goes on. Acting is also terrifying as an experience and requires a helluva lot of self discipline to put yourself on stage at all.

One of the most enjoyable photographs I've ever seen of myself was reading the script for the first time pretty well. We never touched the last couple of scenes at all as I mentioned before so it was with some amazement and some enjoyment it was read before an invited audience of "celebrities" with stage directions read out by no less than Sylvia Syms. There was quite a bit of competition for these parts (we won't go into that) and it wasn't entirely the cast as it became but my part was there having gone though tribulations between other people and the director and away we went but the sheer enjoyment of reading that was exhilarating and a splendid way to begin a delightful short run of this play which was so well received by everybody. As they said, 'The ensemble playing from time to time, was quite magnificent.' Well, that's what you call a pat on the back.

The doll to the left – Kavoliov his name is – I don't remember exactly what he did in the play but I do know one thing for certain – I believe he's gone to a good home. So joy all round.

I've enjoyed Spike Milligan's various performances for a very long time. I remember obviously the Goons which was my regular treat every week on the radio when I was young and I was very impressed with his versatility – Little Dreams of a Scorpion (his poetry) and I did see The Bedsitting Room or something similar with boot hill (a pile of boots) on the stage and I remember one of his theatre performances where he was playing a character (I think it was Oblamov) who couldn't stop sleeping. When the curtain came down about three quarters, he stopped it and said, "It's a bit of a slap in the face. You've been respectful all night and I just say,

Ron Moody and I rehearsing the Gravedigger Scene from Hamlet – directed by Peter Coe, Globe Bankside. By kind permission of Globe Bankside.

'Off you go'. It's not right." He sat on the edge of the stage and kept us entertained for another hour and a half at least which I thought was admirable. Ken Dodd has inherited this habit, I believe.

I've worked with him a few times in a little cartoony sort of way – a spoof Olympics, that kind of thing but when I had the chance of doing this, I was naturally anxious to be in it –'Adolf Hitler, My Part in his Downfall'. It was a toss-up whether I'd be the sort of P.E. instructor or the boxer and I'm so pleased it was decided I would be the boxer and improvise the scene with Jim Dale. There's just an outline of 2 or 3 incidents which happen in the course of the bout and that's all I had and all Jim had and as far as I know that's all the Director had to go on. It was confidence all round. Anyway, the night before was not ideal preparation. I'd been very clever. I went to a hotel near Pinewood, I think it was and had a curry that evening just to stoke up the fires, retired to bed early and was just nicely asleep when the telephone woke me up and then I realised that the bedroom was too hot, way too hot even with the windows open, although it was at least the Autumn and I didn't sleep all night for the heat of the room more than anything else. So, I was high as a kite and full of beans to play the part in an improvised way (had my breakfast with Bob Todd who tactfully kept feeding me bits of the Daily Mirror in the hope that I would shut up and demonstrate my reading age of about 4 and leave him in peace). Eventually we got there. Nothing was repeated at all. We just blazed away all morning, it was amazing. Jim was a joy, both of us on the same wavelength – we both enjoyed it and I think were proud of what we did. Very recently "Adolf Hitler, My Part in his Downfall" was on a tour and they omitted the boxing match which I'm not sure is obeisance or sacrilege.

Spike Milligan. I include a poem about a man who was very difficult but worth it.

MILLIGAN LIVES

Spike Milligan is dead
They frown the naff tributes he predicted –
An unshackled Wit in the pig-thick of it –
His spirit now distils to something less afflicted.
R.I.P. Van Milligoon 1918 (the end of one war) to
2002
It's Spring: CUCKOO!?
Wherever Oil is burned at Midnight
His Voice comes striding on The Wind
Death is full of surprises.

Peter Davidson

This "Hamlet" directed by Peter Coe opened the Globe Theatre, Bankside,as I mentioned, Sam Wannamaker's project by staging the first Shakespeare play on this spot for some 400 years. It was very resourceful. The theatre was PVC and designed and set up I believe by the students of the Royal College of Art. The body of the dead Ophelia was a figure made by Adele Rutstein of Twiggy, the model, which was in Dickens & Jones window so you had the model of a model, a real model presented as a strange new sculpture one can say – fascinating.

What happened was I was one of several tall people chosen to be a soldier in the first instance so I was Barnardo who opens the play seeing the Ghost on the battlements. He then was looking for a second gravedigger to play with Ron Moody and he auditioned these soldiers, including me, getting us to read the "To be or not to be" speech from Hamlet's own mouth and that's what I won and became second gravedigger which was lovely. He

Barnardo with Horatio (Gary Raymond) in a "Ghost Scene" in Hamlet. By kind permission of Globe Bankside.

told us to speak in our own voices and it was suggested we do not wear make-up but we were after contrasts as well naturally, the result being that Ron Moody made himself up as a gravedigger with very death-like make-up and I was just me – hairy. We both wore black boiler suits and a black PVC cap which conveyed "gravediggers crematorium" perhaps. We certainly were an image of death and we pronounced dissatisfaction with what's going on in Elsinore from our very entrance.

The text of the Open University's Hamlet which was used in the Arts Foundation Course became our script which I was now playing in the theatre and, shortly before had taught to the students of the Open University. So it was recognition upon recognition upon recognition but a strange thing, for me at least, was to see Ron Moody play Polonius , not as a bumbling old fool by any means but a Machiavellian figure who manipulated the Court. The whole thing was a great success, it must be said and a Full Cast Recording by Argo was made in a room festooned with microphones which was an additional experience on top of the play itself. To cap it all I think Peter Coe married Inge Borg, the costume designer of the production.

On the lighter side, I did have the opportunity to create the only bit of Shakespeare I ever have wittingly. On one matinee, the Ghost was not there as far as anybody was concerned but we had his music. Horatio went screaming off, having seen a comet perhaps, and everybody else tried to screw themselves into the stage which left me with the entire audience and a pool of silence. While Horatio was finding the Ghost, tilting back in his chair with his feet in the wash basin smoking a cheroot, I wandered around and wondered with the audience eventually, "Methinks 'twas here then," and slowly they began to agree and were more or less happy when the Ghost marched on – tempting to say 'blowing smoke rings' but he honestly wasn't.

He was there with his usual aplomb and nobody ever knew.

A moment of Shakespeare history, gilded by a visit from Katie Hepburn who came to see the show wearing a white suit rather like Hamlet's white mod. suit and, looking us straight in the eye, thanked us for a most exciting production – rare praise indeed. Finally, what distinguished this production was its setting – the Greek Colonels had recently mounted a coup to seize power in Greece – so the audience heard jet transports flying overhead as they enter the auditorium. The soldiers had grenade launchers and so on. It was a broad enough hint without in any way interfering with Shakespeare.

Peter had done a Macbeth set in an African tribe, which apparently was rather telling as well. I should mention here the Macbeth he asked me to be Lennox in which began at Guildford and did a tour of several theatres. We'd studied it at school and I had liked it very much ever since and was delighted to get the chance. His idea for that was to have the stage planked over with half tree trunks cut lengthwise from the footlights right back to the cyclorama, at an angle, it seemed, of 45 degrees. It honestly took us a while to get used to the gradient.) I did have a peek at the production during a scene I wasn't in and it really did work. It was genuinely presented to each individual rather than to the best seat in the house, if you follow – very good. To take that production to illustrate a couple of things, Paul Daneman was Macbeth and Dorothy Tutin was Lady Macbeth and a good time was had by all until the day that somebody said "Macbeth" in the dressing room (which is bad luck) and there is that tradition, or rather requirement that if you do that you go out, turn round 3 times and spit to exorcise the curse then come back in and all will be well. The services of the 'good' witch certainly were called on because someone said Macbeth, was despatched outside to do the ritual but didn't do it all and we all broke into laughter and shrugged it off, sort of thing. Fair enough. But in the second half, there was a scene with a well set in these rough hewn planks and suddenly the whole bloody lot started moving at gathering speed towards the front row of the audience. It was all hands on deck, backs to the mast as it were and we managed to stop it going too far so the stage crew could tighten the bolts to secure it. It really was a very close thing. All they saw, if they saw anything in particular, was the line of the cast grunting in unison. Apparently it wasn't perceived but by God it was perceived by us! Next time we met in the dressing room, we were a bit ashen and I can assure you we will do the whole ritual (or better still never ever say Macbeth again).

The comic moment of that production without a doubt was again involving the well. In the last matinee performance, it's rather a nice tradition that actors do something unnoticeable to the rest of the cast perhaps but certainly unnoticeable to the audience, to make one actor or possibly the whole lot corpse. So there we were round the well, sitting or lolling on the wall, which protruded a couple of feet quite nicely above the stage level, chatting about this and that, probably about Geoff Boycott, the Yorkshire batsman, gazing casually at the surface of the well, when a deep sea diver emerged in the middle of the well from the bottom. He had a flexible tube from the helmet and at the other end was a bulb, a rubber bulb and Duncan, whose strongest point is to be dead was rolling around, as far as his costume would allow, pumping away gleefully at his globe bulb, wearing a grin from ear to ear and back again, with his back to the audience thank God.

CHAPTER 22

THE COMMERCIALS.

I should say something about the commercials I've done because they are virtually 'sonnets at their best.

I remember working for a director for the third time playing a character in Morse, I think it was, and he said to one of the technical directors that he'd chosen me because he wanted someone who could make an immediate impact and the reason was, I'm sure, that he'd directed me in a commercial where you do have to make an "immediate impact". There's no time for faffing around, putting on your lipstick. The other thing is commercials, with a minimum of effort, can get you foreign travel. My provenance is varied. I am legitimately – paradoxically legitimately – descended from the marauding Vikings – if you can see the richness of the texture of that. I've been mistaken for all sorts of nationalities. In Germany I've been mistaken for Russian, in France, I've been mistaken for German and also Scandinavian and I remember once in London, a sharp character tried to offer me 20 naughty photographs in German so a 'man for all seasons' – this is why – with the languages as well – I've been able to go to foreign countries briefly "to make an impact" and come back again none the worse for wear. Keeps the wheels turning and can be very interesting and you meet people briefly to do a job which can be very agreeable. I'm thinking of a couple in particular: I was the works manager for Mercedes

Benz in a commercial we made in Munich so we flew out on Lufthansa and arrived in Munich at about 11 o'clock at night and, as per contract, we were taken to a slap-up dinner by an interpreter I think, who spoke both languages.

Well, we were going to bed at about 1 o'clock in the morning and, as we left the restaurant, they gave us the script which was quite a portfolio I can assure you. I'd done a few commercials by this time and, while the chap next to me went to bed and worried about it and was really a bit of a nervous wreck by the time we did it, I kept my copy firmly shut, went to bed, set the alarm for very early next morning so began my day early and learned it when I was fresh and it was spontaneous. It really did pay off – no cue cards or anything like that. When I came back I was so thrilled to bits with myself, I was given a little bottle of sparkling German wine and a cuddle from the German air hostess whose name was Marcia, if any of you should be so lucky as to meet her.

Coming back, we flew up the Thames past Tower Bridge, The Houses of Parliament and all that jazz and then we were dismissed as the pilot began to descend but she had inveigled me into the cabin and it was absolutely magical – it really was better than 'tele'.

What else? I went to France and did 2 or 3 jobs: I was a Canadian lumberjack in the most horrible plaid shirt you've ever seen which I wore with glee quite a long time afterwards, which reminds me, you can usually buy your costume at a reduced price so I have wonderful snow boots and fisherman's sweaters, all you can imagine – mostly unworn or just for a party. It's a souvenir – "seen it, done it, got the T-shirt."

Back to France. Would you believe it? They wanted someone to be the French Minister of the Interior, in other words the Home Secretary of France to launch a national development in t he French telephone service. The director came to London and of course the fact that I was able to audition from 'bonjour' on, lock stock and barrel in French was a tremendous asset so off I went to find myself doing a kind of spoof of that scene in Dr Strangelove where the Minister is there and his girlfriend rings him up on the military phone and he has to say quietly, "Not today thank you" and continue his briefing. The director himself was an actor but wasn't very good at getting the other side of the camera. He just kept banging away without telling me whether I was on close-up or wide shot or what. You might say I should have asked these things but at that time they were more experienced than I was so it was up to them. But since then, needless to say, I've been playing the part of the Ministre de l'Interieur, quite magnificently in what became my own best suit, to the amazement of people on the tube.

A lunch break in a commercial.

Willie Baxter did me no harm at all – Scott's Porage Oats – we did 3 television and then the voice-over I eventually recorded in Dublin. Everybody over a certain age does remember it. I would love to see the Benny Hill take-off of it. But that's just narcissism… we're supposed to have that aren't we?

I'm glad to sing the praise of good commercials and, need I say, directors of great standing have no problem ducking between fine art and commercials. I've been directed in a commercial by Ridley Scott and by Karel Reisz for example.

It's interesting isn't it? I understand now why we used to scream down to television showrooms at dawn on Monday morning when they showed all the new TV commercials for the week and you saw this wonderful show which was going to star you at some point and there was this captive audience looking through the iron grill, of actors and passers by.

Television can certainly have immediate impact. I remember the Karel Reisz advert I mentioned, was for a butcher. I was to be a Co-op butcher, one of several little vignettes of a baker, a butcher – all to do with things sold at the Co-op so the idea was to be jolly – as he put it, "We shan't be doing any acting today. We shall be exuding bonhomie for 15 seconds."

My job was to demonstrate to a housewife, having established a 'hello', that this superior piece of meat would slice like a dream so I had this hand gesture which was almost balletic so this was duly done and every time I went to my local butcher thereafter, the bloke behind the counter, who was extraordinarily ham fisted, looked at me fair and square in the eye, winked and said, 'Pound of mince guv?' – waving his arms about like a Heathrow parking attendant telling the pilot of an incoming aircraft to try the airport next door. I laughed, he laughed, the whole shop laughed and it sounded as if the whole street laughed so that can't be bad.

CHAPTER 23

THE RIVER.

It would be nice to finish with a Flourish. For that we need to return to France, on holiday this time, where it seems my Mount Parnassus is to be found. You'll remember it was there that the breakthrough Lay of the Lost Nostril was conceived over the course of a year.

A later poem is in many ways the reverse of that. Famously, the title knocked on my bedroom door at about 3.30 a.m.: "THE RIVER".

It seemed, before I had time to even find a rhyme for the first line, I finished the last line and excitedly waited for Maggie to wake up and become compos mentis enough to be impressed.

The facts:

It was written all in one go at the speed of thought.

There are no spelling mistakes and it covers 3 ½ + pages of foolscap.

One word only – "scents" and "perfumes" are interchanged.

It proved to me that poetry is natural to me and remains a defence against those who point fingers at me for failing O level Maths!

THE RIVER

The earth held its breath,
The sun tried not to burn
Then from that sun, the centre of that heaving, hoping earth
there sprang a mountain called Egitica,
thrust forth in a stream of steam and uproarious ash and spume,
Its tumult in frenzy at the amazed low sky.
For eons it rose and could not fall
red and black and ash and smoke and nothing alive at all
to give back for the crack and crack and crack and crescendo
with no diminishing.
For all eternity the earth spewed forth in only one direction,
Forever, there was never an ending to destruction and waste
and heat;
a powerless power, world without end and without beginning.
Then sudden why, stop.
Smoke became rock.
Something out of nothing
Fixed forever.
Black not burning,
Sharp edged not swirling,
No more red, sudden grey,
More dead than before.
But yet an upward striving mountain forever called Egitica.
The amazed, low sky kissed this thing, not imagined before,
kissed the still slight smoking crest, so far and away above the sea,
It gave one cool impossible drop of water
that, uncertain, wisped away, invisible yet surprising.
Then came another such balm to the fleeing heat
and then another, less timorous than before
and then another, now bold and lingering, visible on the face of
the rock like a tear of joy.

This one drop etched for eons,
a slow definite grin in the face of the black hearted rock face
down less lingering.
A slow drop and then another and another drop drips, drips
grinning direct down
the same slit in the infinite rock,
hard, but yet long, soft and yielding rock suddenly smoother
once more swirling as light shines in the water glistens, fed
from above, a drop at a time
now shorter and shorter times between the blessed drops.
Smooth kisses let fall from that same forever giving bounteous
low sky.
Thus, windswept now, clouds clash against the mountain raised
high disdainful
to contemplate its lava plain.
Aloof now, basking in the certainty of ever drops that even now
come for sure
to bathe broadly the mountainside and turn its black, slight green
softer still and glowing cool, then cold and snow and a sudden
rush across it all
Massive, cloaking snow set forever but no,
falls again down the face together a rush of white,
then all light in the sun again and heat from outside.
Thus the river.
Thus its cataract lunges down
fast leaping from splinter to splinter
then sharp crag to next splitting crag
Occasional pool, quick shattered and bigger, falls together
crash to the next
Then again and joined with others dropping tumultuous
together final falling
to the base and right angle of the plain of Egitica
There begin the slow fall of it and others from other sides of the
mountain

Down slower now but wider, almost sliding, through discarded
tumbled rocks obdurate black still,
Until the first timorous reed of definite green and tilting at a
dragonfly, so blue it seemed that all the sky hummed at once on
the tipmost trembling tip of that first green reed,
Knifing into a stray breeze, laden heavy and hot with the ancient
scents of Egitica.
The first fish flops diffident in the shade of a light brown nice
sized rock
but does not deceive its fisher birds spears between its toes and waits
quivering for the next bigger fish, now sure and headed downstream.
Flats of sand interspersed the crumbles of rocks, strewn lightly
by the stream slightly swollen now by other rains and snows
and cataracts and tumultuous waters come too far to here.
More sailing now, clumps of reeds swirl inconsequential, can't
resist the vastly running weather.
On through palm trees thudding their trunks into the sandbanks
too separate to really see
That here, the music from the tents and braying of tethered
animals faster yet and then a wave,
Brown and light brown topped, and full of sand scrapes out yet,
subsiding, fills and fans out and spreads the delta.
Its fingers feel towards, dare not quite embrace but finally consent
The river enwraps itself into the sea and seems to die but does
not but sweeps on yet more mighty, yet deeper, bluer more full
of sun and power
A gentler heaving echo of so long and far ago,
When the earth held its breath and the sun tried not to burn
And one single drop of water elected to become a river and call
itself Egitica.

Peter Davidson

The ball I threw into the air as a child
has not yet reached the ground.
My thanks to Dylan Thomas.

Thanks to Maggie, Mr. ByTheWay's
favourite prompter.

Thanks also to Cedric for the unstinting
technical advice.
Thanks to Nick Theáto.

"My highly regarded DVD presentation."
An Invitation to Contemporary Art

"Goes straight to the heart of the matter - exhilerating."
The Director, Museum of Modern Art, Calais

"This will open a lot of doors for a lot of people."
The Librarian

"Gets onto the right wavelength. I show it to my students."
David Foster, Painter, Art School Senior Lecturer